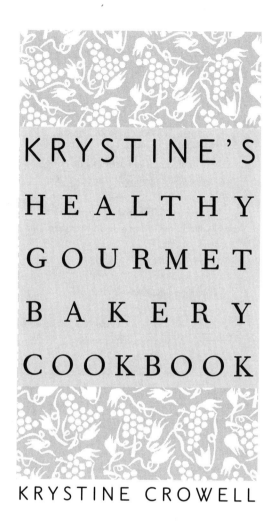

KRYSTINE'S HEALTHY GOURMET BAKERY COOKBOOK

KRYSTINE CROWELL

HP BOOKS

HPBooks
Published by The Berkley Publishing Group
A member of Penguin Putnam Inc.
200 Madison Avenue
New York, NY 10016

Copyright © 1998 by Krystine Crowell
Book design by Bonnie Leon
Cover photograph of the author by Buddy Rosenberg
Cover food photography by Zeva Oelbaum

First edition: March 1998

Published simultaneously in Canada.

The Penguin Putnam Inc. World Wide Web site address is
http://www.penguinputnam.com

Library of Congress Cataloging-in-Publication Data

Crowell, Krystine.
    Krystine's healthy gourmet bakery cookbook / Krystine Crowell.
        p.   cm.
    Includes index.
    ISBN 1-55788-282-7
    1. Baking.   2. Desserts.   3. Low-fat diet—Recipes.   4. Sugar-free
diet—Recipes.   5. Low-cholesterol diet—Recipes.   6. Salt-free
diet—Recipes.   I. Title.
TX765.C89   1998
641.8'15—dc21   97-32732
                                                                 CIP

Printed in the United States of America

10   9   8   7   6   5   4   3   2   1

To the wind beneath my wings:
my children, Michael and Amanda

CONTENTS

ACKNOWLEDGMENTS

There are many people to thank. Each and every one of them has helped make Krystine's Healthy Gourmet Bakery and this cookbook a dream come true. First I would like to thank my amazing family. They are the most important people in my life and without a doubt will stand by my side and support whole-heartedly whatever I do. Thank you, Don Crowell, Jr.—a wise, kind, gentle, fascinating individual who also happens to be my father. Dad, you have helped make all of this possible and I will be forever grateful. To my devoted, loving, fearless mother, who never let me give up. Without her wisdom, love, and guidance I could not have accomplished what I have. Grandma Chizu, you are the most perfect woman I know, every day I strive to become just like you. Thank you for mothering my two children so that I could run my bakeries. No one has contributed to this book more than Todd, my incredibly devoted husband and very best friend. Thank you, thank you for putting up with it all, especially me.

I feel so very fortunate to have the reputable Robert E. Tabian as my literary agent. Thank you, Bob, for all you brought to this book. I would like to express my heartfelt gratitude to John Duff for believing in me. Thank you, John, Michael Kenney, and everyone at The Berkley Publishing Group, who have worked so hard on this project. I truly believe that I am among the luckiest authors to have worked with such a gifted editor, Jeanette Egan. Her nutritional background made an invaluable contribution to this cookbook.

Much appreciation and gratitude go to the following: Head Chef Mario Bonilla, my dear friend and left hand; the bakery could not run so efficiently without him. Paula Amemiya, whose talent and amazing non-fat recipes helped us get off to a great start. Shirley Schutt, manager of the Palos Verdes store, who never let me down. Greg Doran, manager at Brentwood, did an outstanding job; I will always remember the good times we had. Paul Grenier put his heart and soul into the bakery; his devotion and hard work will never be forgotten. Deep heartfelt thanks go to the rest of the staff: Antonio Sanchez, Marriane Jackson, Terry Wilkenson, Mark Hernandez, Michael Buccanon, Buffy Finch, Toshi, George Tamajian, Nati Goday, and the very special Dick Amemiya.

Creating this book was quite a process and a great deal of indebtedness goes to the following people: Sarah and Paul Edwards, who introduced me to the Penguin Putnam group, will never be forgotten. I am obliged to Bin Schutt, Kevin Eng, Tony Gayton, and the brilliant Julie Earley Gayton for their priceless contributions. Special thanks go to Jon Mercedes III, Phillipe Salizar, and Cybil Webb. My humble appreciation goes to the beautiful, brilliant Suzanne Somers and to the talented, ever-so-dashing Dennis Quaid for their comments.

Last of all, I would like to thank all my fabulous, devoted customers; without their love and support none of this could be possible.

My dreams of opening a bakery began in Grandma Ethyl's kitchen. It was there that I became passionate about homemade desserts and sweets. From the time I was seven, I spent every summer with my grandmother. We would cook and bake all day, just the two of us. She patiently taught old family recipes and techniques to her young, enthusiastic student. By the time I reached the age of ten, I could bake cookies, brownies, and cakes better than any adult in my family. I became the designated dessert maker for all family gatherings. In junior high school, my excitement didn't fade. I began entering bake-offs and won blue ribbons for cheesecakes, brownies, and cakes. The neighborhood kids did not come over to my house for milk and my mom's cookies but for milk and Krystine's cookies.

My mother recognized my passion for baking and cooking, and felt I had a special talent. She encouraged me from a young age to "play" in the kitchen; lucky for me she wasn't concerned about the mess left behind.

When I got older and went off to college my mother continued to encourage me. With her support, I was able to get my degree in business with the hope of opening up my own bakery someday. After graduating, however, I put my career goal on hold for a few years. I fell in love, married, and had a beautiful baby boy. The only downside of all this was the seventy-five pounds that came with love and a baby. Unfortunately my passion for sweet desserts did not help.

After a year I was desperate to lose weight. I starved myself and tried every diet on the market. The result was not weight loss, but fatigue, headaches and despair. I knew I had to change my eating habits. I didn't feel healthy and I did not want to be another medical statistic in my family. Unfortunately my family has a history of diabetes, high blood pressure, heart disease, cancer, pulmonary dysfunction, and obesity. My little boy needed a mother in good health—it was time to make a drastic change.

I began reading every health and nutrition book available. I learned about the negative effects, both physical and mental, that sugar and fat can have on the body: fatigue, lack of concentration and energy, weight gain, and increased cholesterol just to name a few. I put it to the test, I began cutting out sugar and fat. Pounds melted away. I had energy like never before. In a year and a half, I went from a size eighteen to a size four. I was more productive, happier, and more confident. But there was still something missing—the delicious homemade desserts I've always loved that were such an important part of my life and that I enjoyed making. What was I to do? The only solution was to come up with my own recipes for nonfat, low-fat, and reduced-fat baked goods. My initial experimental recipes are not worth discussing (or eating for that matter), but after years of trial and error I developed a repertoire of delicious desserts. These included nonfat, reduced fat, low fat, reduced cholesterol, dairy free, sugar free, and recipes that allow for the sweetener of your choice: fructose in place of regular table sugar (sucrose) or sugar made from maple syrup in place of brown sugar.

In 1992, with recipes in hand, I was ready to open my bakery. I was very excited, especially since there were no places in Los Angeles that concentrated on fine nonfat desserts. Because of my specialty I was easily able to attract investors. The only question was where to open my dream bakery. Well, I stumbled onto Brentwood, California, a beautiful tree-lined city, made up of extremely health-conscious people, not to mention beautiful cars, spacious homes, and movie stars. It seemed to be the perfect location for my product.

During the construction of my bakery my life was changing. My dream was coming true on the one hand but that was overshadowed by my three-year-old son being diagnosed with a chronic blood disease. I was devastated and yet I had to juggle the bakery and, most important, to be there for my son. During this time I lived in my son's hospital room, which served as an office for me. This hospital room is where I made some of the most important decisions of my life.

In December of 1993, Krystine's Bakery opened with an overwhelming response. Within two short years, we opened a second store in Palos Verdes Estates, California. At the same time the second store opened, and even more exciting, was the successful surgical procedure my son underwent, a splenectomy, which cured his blood disorder. Shortly after the opening of the Palos Verdes store, talk shows began calling about our nonfat creations. They wanted demonstrations and a taste. After appearing on "The Suzanne Somers Show" the phones went crazy. Grocery stores, health food stores, restaurants, health clubs, coffee houses, yogurt shops—everyone wanted Krystine's Healthy Baked Goods.

This triggered the beginning of our wholesale business. We quickly outgrew our two-hundred-square-foot kitchen and our small retail business, and in 1996 we moved into our expansive kitchen to accommodate our growing business. The final step was this cookbook. I am excited to share all my recipes with all my comrades out there who are passionate for desserts like I am but are also health conscious.

The recipes in this book were created with the novice in mind. As mentioned before, they include nonfat, low-fat, reduced-fat, reduced-cholesterol, dairy-free, and sugar-free recipes that allow for the sweetener of your choice. Many of the recipes have been in my family for generations; all come from the heart and a passion for homemade desserts.

Enjoy!

INGREDIENTS

A Note About Sweeteners

In the four years I have owned the bakery, I have spoken with hundreds of people regarding sugar and its effect on their bodies. Each and every individual is different, and how sugar is absorbed into the bloodstream varies from one person to the next. The most controversy concerning our baked goods is over some of the sweeteners we use. For example, diabetics don't like the fact that we use maple syrup granules in some of our products. Nondiabetics say our cakes sweetened with aspartame are unnatural.

The most controversial issue is fructose vs. regular sugar (sucrose). Most of our customers—doctors, nutritionists, personal weight trainers, professional athletes, and star celebrities—agree that the effect fructose has on their bodies is much better than that of sucrose. Fructose seems to cause glucose to rise more slowly in the bloodstream than sucrose.

Most of our noninsulin diabetic customers have been able to tolerate our baked goods, which are low in sucrose. In any case, whatever sweetener you choose should be a matter of personal preference and the reaction your body has to the various types of sugars. I know many people who eat massive quantities of sucrose and feel perfectly fine afterward. I do not happen to be one of those lucky individuals, and that is why my recipes call for alternatives. If you prefer, my recipes allow you to substitute regular sugar (sucrose) for fructose and brown sugar for maple syrup granules. Pleasing all is my goal and having something for everyone is what I strive for.

Granulated fructose and maple syrup granules are available at natural foods stores and some supermarkets.

Flours

Most of the recipes call for unbleached all-purpose flour, which is available in supermarkets. Other recipes call for whole-wheat flour, whole-wheat pastry flour, and cake flour. Whole-wheat pastry flour, available in natural foods stores, and cake flour are low in gluten. When cutting down the fat in baked goods, always choose a low-gluten or medium-gluten flour, such as all-purpose, rather than bread flour, which is high in gluten. One of the functions of fat in baking is to make the product more tender by interfering with the formation of the gluten strands during mixing. With less fat the product can be tough and dry if a high-gluten flour is used or if the product is overmixed.

Oat bran and rolled oats, both low in gluten, are used in many recipes.

Fruit Purees

Several of the recipes call for applesauce or pureed fruits, including baby food fruits. These fruits replace part of the fat and make the baked goods more moist and tender, as well as adding flavor and natural sugar.

Egg Whites and Egg Substitutes

Egg whites and liquid egg substitutes are used in almost all recipes where eggs are needed. Whole eggs and egg yolks are used infrequently, and only when they are necessary to give the best product. As a quick guide, there are 8 large egg whites in 1 cup. If measuring egg whites, and a whole egg white would be too much, lightly beat the egg white with a fork and use a spoon to add the correct amount to the measuring cup.

Dairy Products

Skim (nonfat) milk, nonfat and low-fat yogurt, nonfat sour cream, nonfat and light cream cheese are used extensively to reduce the amount of fat and cholesterol. Reduced-fat margarine is used when possible. Reduced amounts of butter are added to some recipes for flavor and a better texture.

Other Ingredients

Reduced-fat peanut butter and fruit-sweetened jams are used occasionally to reduce fat and sugar. Nuts and chocolate chips are used in the recipes, but because these are high in fat, the amounts are smaller than in standard recipes.

About the Nutritional Analysis

All recipes were analyzed using a nutritional database. Optional ingredients are not included in the analysis, and if there is a range for the ingredients, the first amount is used in doing the calculations.

MUFFINS, SCONES, AND OTHER BREADS

My favorite morning ritual now consists of gobbling up some freshly baked low-fat goodies, drinking a glass of ice-cold, freshly squeezed orange juice, and sipping a mug of dark-roasted coffee. This is how I love to start my day.

Back in my childhood, however, the ultimate get-up-and-go weekend breakfast would consist of eggs scrambled in pork grease, two strips of crisp bacon, fried hash brown potatoes, and big fluffy homemade biscuits smothered in gravy, all served with an ice-cold glass of whole milk. Of course, during the weekdays there was never enough time to make a feast like this, so my usual breakfast routine before school was a trip to the local doughnut shop where deep-fried apple fritters, rainbow cake doughnuts, and chocolate milk awaited my daily arrival.

In the late eighties, I began seeing muffins at the local doughnut shops. They were supposedly less fattening than doughnuts because they were baked, not fried. Wrong! To my surprise, these baked muffins had approximately 30 grams of fat each. I hate to think how many of those "healthy" muffins I consumed.

In the early nineties, people were, finally, becoming more educated about the foods they were eating, but nowhere could you find a low-fat, let alone nonfat, muffin. This inspired me to create a nonfat muffin. My nonfat muffins were introduced first at the bakery, followed by low-fat scones, nonfat cinnamon rolls, and reduced-fat quick breads. In my quest for perfecting my healthy breakfast treats, I used such ingredients as nonfat yogurt, egg whites, skim milk, fruit puree, and tofu to replace fat and reduce cholesterol.

You will find the recipes in this chapter are delicious and certainly healthier than the traditional American breakfast.

PUMPKIN-GINGERBREAD DROP SCONES

Makes 24 scones

The exceptional combination of pumpkin and spice
is a perfect start to any morning.

PER SCONE
Cal 138
Carb 26 gm
Prot 2 gm
Total fat 3 gm
Sat fat 1 gm
Cal from fat 19%
Chol 7 mg
Sodium 69 mg

2 cups unbleached all-purpose flour

1/3 cup fructose or table sugar (sucrose)

2 1/2 teaspoons baking powder

1 teaspoon ground cinnamon

2 teaspoons ground ginger

1 teaspoon ground nutmeg

1/3 cup butter, softened

2/3 cup canned pumpkin

1/3 cup egg whites or liquid egg substitute

1/3 cup plain nonfat yogurt

Preheat oven to 400F (205C). Spray a baking sheet with vegetable oil spray. In a large bowl, whisk together flour, fructose, baking powder, cinnamon, ginger, and nutmeg. Stir in butter, pumpkin, egg whites, and yogurt to make a thick batter.

Using an ice cream scoop, drop the batter in mounds about 2 inches apart onto prepared baking sheet. Bake 20 to 25 minutes or until lightly browned. Serve warm.

FRESH STRAWBERRY SCONES

Makes 16 scones

These heavenly scones are a must with hot English tea.
Absolutely fabulous!

2 1/2 cups plus 1 tablespoon unbleached
   all-purpose flour
2 teaspoons baking powder
1/2 teaspoon baking soda
1/4 cup fructose or table sugar (sucrose)
4 tablespoons butter, softened

1/4 cup nonfat sour cream
1/3 cup liquid egg substitute
1 teaspoon pure vanilla extract
3/4 cup fresh or frozen strawberries,
   chopped and drained

PER SCONE
Cal 127
Carb 20 gm
Prot 3 gm
Total fat 4 gm
Sat fat 2 gm
Cal from fat 28%
Chol 7 mg
Sodium 109 mg

Preheat oven to 400F (205C). Spray a baking sheet with vegetable oil spray. In a medium bowl, sift together the 2 1/2 cups flour, baking powder, baking soda, and fructose. Work in butter and sour cream with your fingers until dough resembles rolled oats. Add egg substitute and vanilla, and, with your fingers, combine mixture until thoroughly incorporated.

Sprinkle the 1 tablespoon of flour over the strawberries to absorb juice. Add floured strawberries and mix until evenly combined.

Using an ice cream scoop, drop the batter in mounds about 2 inches apart onto prepared baking sheet. Bake 20 to 25 minutes or until lightly browned. Serve warm.

NONFAT WHOLE-WHEAT BLUEBERRY SCONES

Makes 20 scones

When I introduced these scones to the bakery, they became an instant success! Every day customers ordered these by the dozens. They have a wholesome, healthy appearance unlike that of a traditional scone. The blueberries complement the goodness of the whole-wheat flour. This recipe is so easy to prepare and you only have to use one bowl.

1 cup whole-wheat flour
1 1/4 cups plus 2 tablespoons unbleached
   all-purpose flour
1/4 cup fructose or table sugar (sucrose)
2 tablespoons baking powder
1/4 teaspoon salt

1/2 cup plain nonfat yogurt
1/3 cup egg whites or liquid egg substitute
3/4 cup plus 2 tablespoons nonfat
   (skim) milk
1/2 cup fresh or frozen blueberries

Preheat oven to 400F (205C). Spray a baking sheet with vegetable oil spray. In a large bowl, stir together whole-wheat flour, all-purpose flour, fructose, baking powder, and salt. Add yogurt, egg whites, and milk, and, with your fingers, combine mixture until thoroughly incorporated.

Sprinkle the 2 tablespoons of flour over the blueberries to absorb any juice. Add floured blueberries and mix until evenly combined.

Using an ice cream scoop, drop the batter in mounds about 2 inches apart onto prepared baking sheet. Bake 20 to 25 minutes or until lightly browned. Serve warm.

BOYSENBERRY SCONES

Makes 24 scones

Boysenberries are my favorite of all berries. Baked inside a scone, they're irresistible. One bite of these magnificent creations and you will have instant gratification.

PER SCONE
Cal 72
Carb 11 gm
Prot 2 gm
Total fat 2 gm
Sat fat 1 gm
Cal from fat 25%
Chol 5 mg
Sodium 110 mg

2 1/4 cups plus 2 tablespoons unbleached all-purpose flour
1/3 cup fructose or table sugar (sucrose)
2 1/2 teaspoons baking powder
1/2 teaspoon salt

1/4 cup butter, softened
1 cup plain nonfat yogurt
1/4 cup egg whites or liquid egg substitute
1 teaspoon grated lemon rind
1 cup fresh or frozen boysenberries

Preheat oven to 400F (205C). Spray a baking sheet with vegetable oil spray. In a large bowl, stir together the 2 1/4 cups flour, fructose, baking powder, and salt. Add butter, yogurt, egg whites, and lemon rind and, with your fingers, combine mixture until thoroughly incorporated.

Sprinkle the 2 tablespoons of flour onto boysenberries to absorb juice. Add floured boysenberries and mix until evenly combined.

Using an ice cream scoop, drop the batter in mounds about 2 inches apart onto prepared baking sheet. Bake 20 to 25 minutes or until lightly browned. Serve warm.

CHERRY SCONES

Makes 12 scones

PER SCONE
Cal 180
Carb 31 gm
Prot 5 gm
Total fat 4 gm
Sat fat 2 gm
Cal from fat 20%
Chol 10 mg
Sodium 145 mg

There is a subtle taste of sweet cherries in this irresistible English scone. If dried cherries are not available, fresh or frozen ones will work as well.

2 cups unbleached all-purpose flour
1/4 cup fructose or table sugar (sucrose)
2 1/2 teaspoons baking powder
1/4 cup butter, softened
1 cup plain nonfat yogurt
1/3 cup egg whites or liquid egg substitute
1 1/2 teaspoons almond extract
3/4 cup dried cherries

EGG-WASH GLAZE
2 egg whites
2 teaspoons fructose or table sugar (sucrose)

Preheat oven to 400F (205C). Spray a baking sheet with vegetable oil spray. Into a medium bowl, sift together flour, fructose, and baking powder. Work in butter, yogurt, egg whites, almond extract, and cherries with your fingers and knead until mixture is combined.

Pat or roll dough into a 7-inch circle. Cut into 12 wedges. Arrange wedges on prepared baking sheet about 1 inch apart.

For glaze: Whisk together egg whites and fructose, then brush lightly on top of each wedge. Bake scones 12 minutes or until lightly browned. Serve warm.

PAPAYA-MANGO SCONES

Makes 24 scones

An exotic blend of tropical fruits, coconut, and macadamias make this an unforgettable treat from paradise.

PER SCONE
Cal 103
Carb 16 gm
Prot 2 gm
Total fat 3 gm
Sat fat 2 gm
Cal from fat 26%
Chol 7 mg
Sodium 73 mg

2 1/2 cups unbleached all-purpose flour
1/3 cup fructose or table sugar (sucrose)
2 1/2 teaspoons baking powder
1/3 cup butter, softened
1 cup plain nonfat yogurt
1/4 cup egg whites or liquid egg substitute

3/4 cup diced fresh or frozen mango
1/2 cup diced fresh papaya
1/2 cup sweetened flaked coconut
3/4 cup macadamia nuts (optional), chopped

Preheat oven to 400F (205C). Spray a baking sheet with vegetable oil spray. In a large bowl, stir together flour, fructose, and baking powder. Add butter, yogurt, and egg whites and, with your hands, combine mixture until thoroughly incorporated. Add mango, papaya, coconut, and macadamia nuts and mix until evenly combined.

Using an ice cream scoop, drop the batter in mounds about 2 inches apart onto prepared baking sheet. Bake 20 to 25 minutes or until lightly browned. Serve warm.

LEMON-POPPY SEED SCONES

Makes 16 scones

The true English scones are pronounced sk-gones. *My version of these buttery, lemon-flavored delights (made with about half the fat and cholesterol as the English version) will thrill all who try them, even English chaps.*

2 1/2 cups unbleached all-purpose flour
2 teaspoons baking powder
1/2 teaspoon baking soda
1/4 cup fructose or table sugar (sucrose)
4 tablespoons butter, softened

1/4 cup nonfat cottage cheese, drained
1/3 cup liquid egg substitute
1 1/2 tablespoons lemon extract
2 teaspoons freshly grated lemon rind
1 1/2 tablespoons poppy seeds

Preheat oven to 400F (250C). Spray a baking sheet with vegetable oil spray. Into a medium bowl, sift together flour, baking powder, baking soda, and fructose. Work in butter and cottage cheese with your hands until dough resembles rolled oats. Mix in egg substitute, lemon extract, lemon rind, and poppy seeds. Knead with your fingers until thoroughly combined.

With your hands, roll dough into small golf ball–size balls, then flatten to 1/2-inch thickness. Place on prepared baking sheet about 2 inches apart and bake 10 minutes or until lightly browned. Serve warm.

LOW-FAT ORANGE CHEESECAKE MUFFINS

Makes 18 muffins

Oranges and cheesecake in a low-fat muffin—this is truly a match made in heaven. The freshly squeezed orange juice really makes this muffin superb.

PER SCONE
Cal 129
Carb 25 gm
Prot 4 gm
Total fat 1 gm
Sat fat 0 gm
Cal from fat 7%
Chol 2 mg
Sodium 202 mg

3 cups unbleached all-purpose flour
5 teaspoons baking powder
1/2 teaspoon salt
1/2 cup reduced-fat cream cheese
1/2 cup fructose or table sugar (sucrose)

2/3 cup egg whites or liquid egg substitute
1 cup freshly squeezed orange juice
1 cup water
2 tablespoons freshly grated orange rind
1 teaspoon pure vanilla extract

Preheat oven to 350F (175C). Spray a 12-cup muffin pan and a 6-cup muffin pan with vegetable oil spray. Into a small bowl, sift together flour, baking powder, and salt; set aside.

In a large bowl, beat together cream cheese and fructose with an electric mixer until light and creamy. Add egg whites, orange juice, water, orange rind, vanilla, and flour mixture; beat until thoroughly combined, about 1 minute. Do not overbeat.

Spoon batter into prepared muffin cups. Bake 25 minutes or until a wooden pick inserted into the muffin centers comes out clean. Turn out muffins onto a wire rack to cool.

CHOCOLATE CARROT-OAT BRAN MUFFINS

Makes 12 muffins

PER MUFFIN
Cal 274
Carb 45 gm
Prot 4 gm
Total fat 11 gm
Sat fat 1 gm
Cal from fat 36%
Chol 0 mg
Sodium 113 mg

My kids love these! They taste just like chocolate cake but have the healthy goodness of carrots and a touch of oat bran for extra fiber. The carrots and oat bran are undetectable, but I feel good knowing they are there.

3/4 cup unbleached all-purpose flour
3/4 cup whole-wheat pastry flour
  (see Note, below)
1/4 cup unsweetened cocoa powder
1 teaspoon baking soda
1 teaspoon baking powder
1/2 teaspoon ground cinnamon

3/4 cup fructose or table sugar (sucrose)
1/4 cup vegetable oil
1/3 cup egg whites or liquid egg substitute
3/4 cup unsweetened applesauce
1/2 cup oat bran
1 1/2 cups shredded carrots
1 cup chocolate chips

Preheat oven to 350F (175C). Spray a 12-cup muffin pan with vegetable oil spray. In a medium bowl, stir together flours, cocoa, baking soda, baking powder, and cinnamon; set aside.

In a large bowl, beat fructose, oil, egg whites, applesauce, and oat bran with an electric mixer until combined. Stir in flour mixture until combined, about 1 minute. Fold in carrots and chocolate chips.

Spoon batter into prepared muffin cups. Bake 25 minutes or until a wooden pick inserted into the muffin centers comes out clean. Turn out muffins onto a wire rack to cool.

NOTE
Whole-wheat pastry flour is available in natural foods stores.

CARROT-APPLE-
BANANA MUFFINS

Makes 18 muffins

Better known as Morning Glory Muffins at the bakery, these fresh fruit and carrot wonders have a touch of oat bran for that extra fiber we could all use.

3 cups unbleached all-purpose flour

2 teaspoons cornstarch

2 1/2 teaspoons baking powder

2 teaspoons ground cinnamon

3/4 cup butter, softened

3/4 cup maple syrup granules or
    granulated brown sugar

3/4 cup fructose or table sugar (sucrose)

1 cup egg whites or liquid egg substitute

3/4 cup plain nonfat yogurt

2 cups mashed ripe bananas

1 cup shredded carrots

1 cup diced Granny Smith apples

3/4 cup chopped walnuts

PER MUFFIN
Cal 281
Carb 41 gm
Prot 5 gm
Total fat 11 gm
Sat fat 5 gm
Cal from fat 35%
Chol 20 mg
Sodium 159 mg

Preheat oven to 350F (175C). Spray a 12-cup muffin pan and a 6-cup muffin pan with vegetable oil spray. Into a small bowl, sift together flour, cornstarch, baking powder, and cinnamon; set aside.

In a large bowl, beat butter, maple syrup granules, and fructose with an electric mixer until light and creamy. Add egg whites, yogurt, and bananas and beat until smooth. Add flour mixture to banana mixture and stir until blended. Fold in carrots, apples, and walnuts.

Spoon batter into prepared muffin cups. Bake 25 minutes or until a wooden pick inserted into the muffin centers comes out clean. Turn out muffins onto a wire rack to cool.

GOLDEN RAISIN-
ORANGE BRAN MUFFINS

Makes 24 muffins

PER MUFFIN
Cal 211
Carb 38 gm
Prot 6 gm
Total fat 5 gm
Sat fat 2 gm
Cal from fat 21%
Chol 10 mg
Sodium 227 mg

This classic muffin is a great way to begin your morning. It's full of fiber and the goodness of plump golden raisins flavored with freshly squeezed orange juice.
I like to make these jumbo size. If you prefer a smaller muffin, reduce the baking time by 10 minutes. Leftover muffins can be frozen up to 3 months.

3 1/4 cups whole-wheat flour

2 teaspoons baking soda

2 teaspoons baking powder

1/2 cup butter, softened

1 cup maple syrup granules or
    granulated brown sugar

1/2 cup fructose or table sugar (sucrose)

1 cup unsweetened applesauce

1 cup egg whites or liquid egg substitute

1/2 cup freshly squeezed orange juice

1 teaspoon pure vanilla extract

1/2 cup blackstrap molasses

2 cups nonfat (skim) milk

2 tablespoons vinegar

3 cups bran cereal flakes

2 cups rolled oats

Preheat oven to 350F (175C). Spray 2 (12-cup) large muffin pans with vegetable oil spray. In a small bowl, stir together flour, baking soda, and baking powder; set aside.

In a large bowl, beat butter, maple syrup granules, fructose, applesauce, egg whites, orange juice, vanilla, molasses, milk, and vinegar with an electric mixer until thoroughly combined. Add flour mixture to applesauce mixture and stir until incorporated. Stir in bran flakes and oats.

Spoon batter into prepared muffin cups. Bake 30 to 35 minutes or until a wooden pick inserted into the muffin centers comes out clean. Turn out muffins onto a wire rack to cool.

NOTE

If you only have one large muffin pan, refrigerate batter while baking the first batch of muffins.

MANDARIN ORANGE–CHOCOLATE CHIP MUFFINS

Makes 12 muffins

This gratifying combination of orange and rich chocolate will send your taste buds soaring to new heights. Great for breakfast or any time of the day.

PER MUFFIN
Cal 337
Carb 56 gm
Prot 5 gm
Total fat 11 gm
Sat fat 5 gm
Cal from fat 29%
Chol 21 mg
Sodium 177 mg

2 1/2 cups unbleached all-purpose flour
2 1/2 teaspoons baking powder
1 teaspoon ground cinnamon
1/2 cup butter, softened
1 1/4 cups fructose or table sugar (sucrose)
1/2 cup egg whites or liquid egg substitute

3/4 cup plain nonfat yogurt
1/2 cup freshly squeezed orange juice
3/4 cup chopped mandarin oranges, drained
3/4 cup chocolate chips

Preheat oven to 350F (175C). Spray a 12-cup muffin pan with vegetable oil spray. Into a medium bowl, sift together flour, baking powder and cinnamon; set aside.

In a large bowl, beat butter and fructose with an electric mixer until light and creamy. Beat in egg whites, yogurt, and orange juice until smooth. Add flour mixture to yogurt mixture and stir until blended. Fold in oranges and chocolate chips.

Spoon batter into prepared muffin cups. Bake 25 minutes or until a wooden pick inserted into the muffin centers comes out clean. Turn out muffins onto a wire rack to cool.

BLUEBERRY-TOFU
CORN MUFFINS

Makes 8 muffins

Versatile muffins that can be served with breakfast, lunch, or dinner. They are made with corn, fresh plump blueberries, and for a healthy addition, cholesterol-free tofu.

1 1/2 cups unbleached all-purpose flour
1 cup yellow cornmeal
1 tablespoon baking powder
1/2 teaspoon salt
1/2 cup butter, softened
1/2 cup maple syrup granules or
   granulated brown sugar

1/3 cup mashed tofu
1 cup water
1/2 cup canned or frozen whole-kernel corn
1/2 cup fresh or frozen blueberries

Preheat oven to 350F (175C). Spray 8 muffin cups with vegetable oil spray. In a medium bowl, stir together flour, cornmeal, baking powder, and salt; set aside.

In a large bowl, beat butter, maple syrup granules, tofu, and water with an electric mixer until thoroughly blended. Add flour mixture to butter mixture and stir until incorporated. Fold in corn and blueberries.

Spoon batter into prepared muffin cups. Bake 25 minutes or until a wooden pick inserted into the muffin centers comes out clean. Turn out muffins onto a wire rack to cool.

LOW-FAT CHERRY
CHEESECAKE MUFFINS

Makes 12 muffins

Intense in flavor, perfected in texture, this cheese-flavored cake has bits of cherries in every bite—a favorite at the bakery.

2 1/4 cups unbleached all-purpose flour
2 teaspoons baking powder
1/4 teaspoon salt
1/3 cup nonfat cream cheese, softened
2 tablespoons butter, softened
1 cup fructose or table sugar (sucrose)

1/3 cup egg whites or liquid egg substitute
1/2 cup plain nonfat yogurt
1/3 cup freshly squeezed orange juice
1 teaspoon pure vanilla extract
3/4 cup fresh or canned pitted cherries

PER MUFFIN
Cal 216
Carb 48 gm
Prot 5 gm
Total fat 2 gm
Sat fat 1 gm
Cal from fat 8%
Chol 6 mg
Sodium 172 mg

Preheat oven to 350F (175C). Spray a 12-cup muffin pan with vegetable oil spray. Into a small bowl, sift together flour, baking powder, and salt; set aside.

In a large bowl, beat cream cheese, butter, fructose, egg whites, yogurt, orange juice, and vanilla with an electric mixer until thoroughly blended. Add flour mixture to yogurt mixture and stir until incorporated. Fold in cherries.

Spoon batter into prepared muffin cups. Bake 25 minutes or until a wooden pick inserted into the muffin centers comes out clean. Turn out muffins onto a wire rack to cool.

LOW-FAT BUTTERMILK DOUGHNUT MUFFINS

Makes 12 muffins

PER MUFFIN
Cal 171
Carb 33 gm
Prot 4 gm
Total fat 2 gm
Sat fat 1 gm
Cal from fat 10%
Chol 5 mg
Sodium 69 mg

I go crazy over the taste of real buttermilk doughnuts, but since they have approximately 15 to 20 grams of fat per serving, I very seldom indulge. I came up with these impostors to satisfy my craving. These muffins have very little fat and taste like the real thing.

2 cups unbleached all-purpose flour
1 teaspoon baking powder
1 teaspoon baking soda
1/4 teaspoon salt
1 1/2 teaspoons ground nutmeg
2 tablespoons butter or margarine, softened

3/4 cup fructose or table sugar (sucrose)
1/4 cup plain nonfat yogurt
1/2 cup egg whites or liquid egg substitute
1 cup nonfat (skim) milk
1 teaspoon pure vanilla extract

Preheat to 325F (165C). Spray a 12-cup muffin pan with vegetable oil spray. Into a medium bowl, sift together flour, baking powder, baking soda, salt, and nutmeg; set aside.

In a large bowl, beat butter, fructose, yogurt, egg whites, milk, and vanilla with an electric mixer until light and creamy. Add flour mixture to yogurt mixture and stir until thoroughly combined.

Spoon batter into prepared muffin cups. Bake 25 minutes or until a wooden pick inserted into muffin centers comes out clean. Turn out muffins onto a wire rack to cool.

LOW-FAT
COFFEECAKE MUFFINS

Makes 12 muffins

These easy-to-make muffins certainly do not lack the seductive taste of a rich, buttery cinnamon—sour cream coffeecake. What is lacking is all the fat and cholesterol found in the traditional recipe. A maple-cinnamon filling embedded in each center perfectly complements these low-fat crumb cakes.

PER MUFFIN
Cal 244
Carb 53 gm
Prot 4 gm
Total fat 1 gm
Sat fat 0.6 gm
Cal from fat 3%
Chol 5 mg
Sodium 110 mg

Maple-Cinnamon Filling and Topping
   (see opposite)
2 cups unbleached all-purpose flour
2 teaspoons baking powder
1 tablespoon butter, softened
1 cup fructose or table sugar (sucrose)
1 cup nonfat sour cream
1/2 cup egg whites or liquid egg substitute
1 teaspoon pure vanilla extract

MAPLE-CINNAMON FILLING AND
TOPPING
3/4 cup maple syrup granules or
   granulated brown sugar
1/4 cup fructose or table sugar (sucrose)
2 teaspoons ground cinnamon

Preheat oven to 350F (175C). Spray a 12-cup muffin pan with vegetable oil spray. Make filling and topping: In a small bowl, combine maple syrup granules, fructose, and cinnamon; set aside.

Into a medium bowl, sift together flour and baking powder; set aside. In a large bowl, beat butter, fructose, sour cream, egg whites, and vanilla with an electric mixer until incorporated. Add flour mixture to sour cream mixture and stir until thoroughly combined.

Spoon half of the batter into prepared muffin cups, sprinkle with about half of cinnamon mixture, and top with remaining batter. Sprinkle tops of muffins with remaining cinnamon mixture. Bake 25 minutes or until a wooden pick inserted into the muffin centers comes out clean. Turn out muffins onto a wire rack to cool.

FRESH PEACH MUFFINS

Makes 24 muffins

PER MUFFIN
Cal 149
Carb 24 gm
Prot 3 gm
Total fat 5 gm
Sat fat 1 gm
Cal from fat 30%
Chol 0 mg
Sodium 198 mg

This is one of my seasonal muffins at the bakery. I prefer using fresh ripe peaches at the peak of the season, but canned or frozen will do.

2 cups unbleached all-purpose flour
2 cups whole-wheat pastry flour
1 tablespoon baking powder
1 tablespoon baking soda
1/2 teaspoon salt
1 teaspoon ground nutmeg
1 teaspoon ground cinnamon

1/2 cup vegetable oil
1/4 cup baby-food peaches or
    unsweetened applesauce
3/4 cup fructose or table sugar (sucrose)
1/2 cup egg whites or liquid egg substitute
1 cup freshly squeezed orange juice
2 cups chopped peaches

Preheat oven to 350F (175C). Spray 2 (12-cup) muffin pans with vegetable oil spray. Into a medium bowl, sift together flours, baking powder, baking soda, salt, nutmeg, and cinnamon; set aside.

In a large bowl, beat oil, baby-food peaches, fructose, egg whites, orange juice, and chopped peaches with an electric mixer until light and creamy. Add flour mixture to peach mixture and stir until thoroughly combined.

Spoon batter into prepared muffin cups. Bake 25 minutes or until a wooden pick inserted into the muffin centers comes out clean. Turn out muffins onto a wire rack to cool.

LOW-FAT BANANA MUFFINS

Makes 24 muffins

Dense, moist, flavorful, delicious, and low-fat—what more could you ask for? They also freeze well and can be kept up to 2 months in the freezer if wrapped and sealed airtight.

PER MUFFIN
Cal 182
Carb 38 gm
Prot 5 gm
Total fat 1 gm
Sat fat 0 gm
Cal from fat 5%
Chol 0 mg
Sodium 138 mg

2 cups unbleached all-purpose flour
2 cups whole-wheat pastry flour
1 1/2 teaspoons baking powder
1 1/2 teaspoons baking soda
2 cups fructose or table sugar (sucrose)
1 cup nonfat cottage cheese, drained

2 tablespoons vegetable oil
1 tablespoon pure vanilla extract
2 cups mashed ripe bananas
1 1/2 cups egg whites or liquid egg
   substitute

Preheat oven to 350F (175C). Spray 2 (12-cup) muffin pans with vegetable oil spray. Into a large bowl, sift together flours, baking powder, baking soda, and salt; set aside.

In another large bowl, beat fructose, cottage cheese, oil, vanilla, bananas, and egg whites with an electric mixer until light and creamy. Add flour mixture to banana mixture and stir until thoroughly combined, about 1 minute.

Spoon batter into prepared muffin cups. Bake 25 minutes or until a wooden pick inserted into the muffin centers comes out clean. Turn out muffins onto a wire rack to cool.

APPLE CRUMBLE MUFFINS

Makes 12 muffins

There's nothing quite like the combination of fresh apples, cinnamon, and nuts in a supermoist muffin. The crumb topping makes them exceptionally delicious. They are even better the second day, after the flavors have had a chance to blend together.

Crumble Topping (see opposite)
1 cup unbleached all-purpose flour
1/2 cup whole-wheat flour
1 teaspoon baking powder
1/2 teaspoon salt
1/2 teaspoon ground cinnamon
1/2 teaspoon ground allspice
1 cup fructose or table sugar (sucrose)
1/2 cup vegetable oil
1/4 cup unsweetened applesauce
1/2 cup egg whites or liquid egg substitute
1 1/2 cups peeled, diced Granny Smith apples
1/2 cup walnuts (optional), chopped

CRUMBLE TOPPING

4 tablespoons butter, chilled
2/3 cup fructose or table sugar (sucrose)
1/2 cup unbleached all-purpose flour
1 teaspoon ground cinnamon
1/3 cup rolled oats
1/2 cup walnuts, chopped

Preheat oven to 350F (175C). Spray a 12-cup muffin pan with vegetable oil spray. Make topping: In a small bowl, combine all topping ingredients and mix with your fingers until combined; set aside.

In a small bowl, stir together flours, baking powder, salt, cinnamon, and allspice; set aside. In a large bowl, beat fructose, oil, applesauce, and egg whites until thoroughly combined. Add flour mixture to applesauce mixture and beat until smooth, about 1 minute. Fold in apples and walnuts. Spoon batter into prepared muffin cups.

Sprinkle reserved topping on each muffin top with a teaspoon. Bake 25 minutes or until a wooden pick inserted into muffin centers comes out clean. Turn out onto a wire rack to cool.

PUMPKIN-TOFU MUFFINS

Makes 12 muffins

Tofu replaces eggs in these wonderfully moist and slightly spicy muffins. Pumpkin and applesauce add moistness and flavor to this protein-rich treat.

2 cups unbleached all-purpose flour
1 teaspoon baking soda
1 teaspoon ground cinnamon
1/2 cup butter, softened
1 cup fructose or table sugar (sucrose)

1/2 cup unsweetened applesauce
1 cup mashed tofu
1 cup canned pumpkin
3/4 cup pecans (optional), chopped

PER MUFFIN
Cal 249
Carb 39 gm
Prot 4 gm
Total fat 9 gm
Sat fat 5 gm
Cal from fat 32%
Chol 20 mg
Sodium 148 mg

Preheat oven to 325F (165C). Spray a 12-cup muffin pan with vegetable oil spray. Into a small bowl, sift together flour, baking soda, and cinnamon; set aside.

In a large bowl, beat butter, fructose, applesauce, tofu, and pumpkin with an electric mixer until light and creamy. Add flour mixture to pumpkin mixture and beat until combined, about 1 minute. Stir in pecans, if using.

Spoon batter into prepared muffin cups. Bake 25 minutes or until a wooden pick inserted into the muffin centers comes out clean. Turn out muffins onto a wire rack to cool.

LOW-FAT STRAWBERRY YOGURT MUFFINS

Makes 12 muffins

PER MUFFIN
Cal 180
Carb 34 gm
Prot 4 gm
Total fat 3 gm
Sat fat 2 gm
Cal from fat 15%
Chol 6 mg
Sodium 197 mg

This particular muffin is extremely popular and our biggest seller among our wholesale accounts. It's light and fluffy, with plump strawberries throughout.

2 cups unbleached all-purpose flour
2 teaspoons baking powder
2 tablespoons butter, softened
3/4 cup fructose or table sugar (sucrose)

1/2 cup egg whites or liquid egg substitute
1/4 cup nonfat sour cream
3/4 cup low-fat strawberry yogurt
1 cup fresh or frozen strawberries, chopped

Preheat oven to 350F (175C). Spray a 12-cup muffin pan with vegetable oil spray. In a small bowl, sift together flour and baking powder; set aside.

In a large bowl, beat butter, fructose, egg whites, sour cream, and yogurt until light and creamy. Add flour mixture to yogurt mixture and stir until combined. Fold in strawberries.

Spoon batter into prepared muffin cups. Bake 25 minutes or until a wooden pick inserted into the muffin centers comes out clean. Turn out muffins onto a wire rack to cool.

CHOCOLATE-ESPRESSO FREAKOUT MUFFINS

Makes 12 muffins

A sinfully rich-tasting muffin with a crumb topping and chocolate chips in every bite. A hint of coffee complements the chocolate quite nicely.

PER MUFFIN
Cal 354
Carb 49 gm
Prot 6 gm
Total fat 15 gm
Sat fat 7 gm
Cal from fat 38%
Chol 31 mg
Sodium 240 mg

Crumb Topping (see opposite)
2 1/4 cups unbleached all-purpose flour
1/4 cup unsweetened cocoa powder
2 teaspoons baking powder
1/2 teaspoon baking soda
1/2 cup butter, softened
1/4 cup maple syrup granules or
    granulated brown sugar
1/2 cup egg whites or liquid egg substitute
1 cup nonfat chocolate or plain yogurt
1/4 cup espresso or strong coffee
1/2 cup chocolate chips

CRUMB TOPPING
4 tablespoons butter, chilled
1/2 cup unbleached all-purpose flour
2/3 cup fructose or table sugar (sucrose)
1 teaspoon ground cinnamon
1/2 cup chocolate chips
1/2 cup macadamia nuts (optional),
    chopped

Preheat oven to 350F (175C). Spray a 12-cup muffin pan with vegetable oil spray. Make topping: In a small bowl, combine topping ingredients and mix with your fingers until combined; set aside.

In another small bowl, sift together flour, cocoa, baking powder, and baking soda; set aside. In a large bowl, beat butter and maple syrup granules with an electric mixer until light and creamy. Add egg whites, yogurt, and coffee and beat until combined. Add flour mixture and chocolate chips to yogurt mixture and stir until combined.

Spoon batter into prepared muffin cups. Sprinkle topping on each muffin top with a teaspoon. Bake 25 minutes or until a wooden pick inserted in muffin centers comes out clean. Turn out muffins onto a wire rack to cool.

RASPBERRY STREUSEL MUFFINS

Makes 12 muffins

PER MUFFIN
Cal 359
Carb 59 gm
Prot 5 gm
Total fat 12 gm
Sat fat 7 gm
Cal from fat 30%
Chol 31 mg
Sodium 200 mg

This is my favorite of all muffins. The combination of white cake and raspberries with a crisp cinnamon crumb topping makes these tea cake muffins an absolute "must try."

Streusel Topping (see opposite)
2 cups plus 1 tablespoon unbleached
   all-purpose flour
2 teaspoons baking powder
1/2 cup butter, softened
1 cup fructose or table sugar (sucrose)
1 cup nonfat raspberry or vanilla yogurt
1/2 cup egg whites or liquid egg substitute
1 teaspoon pure vanilla extract
1 cup fresh or frozen raspberries

STREUSEL TOPPING
4 tablespoons butter, chilled
1/2 cup unbleached all-purpose flour
2/3 cup fructose or table sugar (sucrose)
1/2 teaspoon ground cinnamon

Preheat oven to 375F (190C). Spray a 12-cup muffin pan with vegetable oil spray. Make topping: In a small bowl, combine topping ingredients and mix with your fingers until combined.

In another small bowl, sift together the 2 cups of flour and baking powder; set aside. In a medium bowl, beat butter and fructose with an electric mixer until light and creamy. Add yogurt, egg whites, and vanilla and mix until combined.

In a small bowl, sprinkle the 1 tablespoon of flour over raspberries and gently toss together. Combine flour mixture with yogurt mixture and stir until combined. Fold in raspberries.

Spoon batter into prepared muffin cups. Sprinkle topping on each muffin top with a teaspoon. Bake 25 minutes or until a wooden pick inserted in center comes out clean.

LOW-FAT APPLE-OAT BRAN MUFFINS

Makes 12 muffins

These wonderfully wholesome muffins, loaded with fruit and fiber, are a great way to start your day! Most of their sweetness comes from apple juice and applesauce.

1 cup oat bran
1/2 cup nonfat (skim) milk
1 1/2 cups unbleached all-purpose flour
2 1/2 teaspoons baking powder
1/2 teaspoon ground cinnamon
1/2 teaspoon ground nutmeg
2 tablespoons nonfat sour cream

1/2 cup unsweetened applesauce
1/2 cup apple juice
1/3 cup apple juice concentrate
1/2 cup egg whites or liquid egg substitute
1/3 cup fructose or table sugar (sucrose)
1 cup diced Granny Smith apple

Preheat oven to 350F (175C). Spray a 12-cup muffin pan with vegetable oil spray. In a small bowl, mix milk with oat bran; set aside. In another small bowl, sift together flour, baking powder, cinnamon, and nutmeg; set aside.

In a large bowl, whisk together sour cream, applesauce, apple juice, apple juice concentrate, egg whites, and fructose until thoroughly combined. Add bran and flour mixtures to applesauce mixture and whisk until combined. Stir in diced apple.

Spoon batter into prepared muffin cups. Bake 30 to 35 minutes or until a wooden pick inserted into the muffin centers comes out clean. Turn out muffins onto a wire rack to cool.

FRESH BLUEBERRY MUFFINS

Makes 12 muffins

PER MUFFIN
Cal 227
Carb 41 gm
Prot 4 gm
Total fat 5 gm
Sat fat 3 gm
Cal from fat 20%
Chol 14 mg
Sodium 183 mg

These soft, crumbly, melt-in-your-mouth muffins come from a recipe that took years to perfect. I am now very proud to introduce to you "the perfect blueberry muffin." Your taste buds will applaud you loudly!

2 cups fresh blueberries
2 cups unbleached all-purpose flour
4 teaspoons baking powder
1 cup fructose or table sugar (sucrose)

1/3 cup butter, softened
1/4 cup liquid egg substitute or egg whites
1 cup nonfat (skim) milk

Preheat oven to 375F (190C). Line a 12-cup muffin pan with paper liners. In a small bowl, coat fresh blueberries by lightly tossing them in 2 tablespoons of the flour; set aside.

In a large bowl, sift together remaining flour, baking powder, and fructose. Add softened butter and cut in with a pastry blender until crumbly. Add egg substitute and milk and stir until blended. Fold in blueberries.

Spoon batter into paper-lined muffin cups. Bake about 35 to 45 minutes or until a wooden pick inserted into the muffin centers comes out clean. Turn out muffins onto a wire rack to cool.

CRANBERRY-BANANA MUFFINS

Makes about 20 muffins

Sweet bananas and tangy cranberries fill these delightfully fluffy muffins.
Toasted walnuts really add a tasty and toothsome flourish.

PER MUFFIN
Cal 202
Carb 29 gm
Prot 5 gm
Total fat 7 gm
Sat fat 3 gm
Cal from fat 31%
Chol 13 mg
Sodium 161 mg

3 1/2 cups unbleached all-purpose flour
2 teaspoons baking soda
1/2 cup unsalted butter, softened
1/4 cup unsweetened applesauce
3/4 cup apple or white grape juice
   concentrate
2 1/2 cups mashed ripe bananas

1 cup liquid egg substitute or egg whites
3/4 cup nonfat plain yogurt
3/4 cup fresh or frozen cranberries,
   chopped
1/2 cup walnuts, roasted (see Note below)
   and chopped

Preheat oven to 375F (190C). Spray 20 muffin cups with vegetable oil spray. Into a small bowl, sift together flour and baking soda; set aside.

In a large bowl, beat butter, applesauce, and juice concentrate together until light. Add bananas, egg substitute, and yogurt and beat with an electric mixer until smooth. Add cranberries, walnuts, and flour mixture to banana mixture and stir until thoroughly combined.

Spoon batter into prepared muffin cups. Bake about 25 to 30 minutes or until a wooden pick inserted into the muffin centers comes out clean. Turn out muffins onto a wire rack to cool.

NOTE

Spread walnuts in a pie pan. Toast in a preheated 350F (175C) oven 5 minutes or until lightly browned. Flaked coconut can also be toasted this way, as can other nuts. Chopped nuts and coconut toast more evenly if stirred at least once.

LEMON LOVE
NOTE MUFFINS

Makes about 12 muffins

PER MUFFIN
Cal 210
Carb 38 gm
Prot 5 gm
Total fat 4 gm
Sat fat 2 gm
Cal from fat 17%
Chol 11 mg
Sodium 169 mg

With freshly grated lemon rind in every bite and a terrific tangy lemon glaze your tummy will sing for joy.

2 1/2 cups unbleached all-purpose flour
1 teaspoon baking soda
1 teaspoon baking powder
1/4 cup fructose or table sugar (sucrose)
1/2 cup egg whites or liquid egg substitute
1 1/4 cups plain nonfat yogurt
1/4 cup unsalted butter, softened
1 teaspoon lemon extract
1 tablespoon freshly grated lemon rind
1 teaspoon pure vanilla extract

GLAZE
1/2 cup fructose or powdered sugar
1/2 cup fresh lemon juice

Preheat oven to 350F (175C). Line a 12-cup muffin pan with paper liners. In a large bowl, sift together flour, baking soda, and baking powder; set aside.

In a large bowl, beat together fructose, egg whites, yogurt, butter, lemon extract, lemon rind, and vanilla with an electric mixer until light. Add flour mixture to yogurt mixture and stir until incorporated.

Spoon batter into paper-lined muffin cups. Bake 25 to 35 minutes or until a wooden pick inserted into muffin centers comes out clean.

Meanwhile, make glaze while muffins are baking: In a small bowl, stir together fructose and lemon juice. Drizzle glaze over warm muffins, using a teaspoon. Turn out muffins onto a wire rack to cool.

APPLE-TOFU NUT BREAD

Makes 2 loaves; 20 slices

Fresh apples, tofu, and a hint of spice make this exceptionally moist bread simply divine.

PER SLICE
Cal 258
Carb 37 gm
Prot 3 gm
Total fat 11 gm
Sat fat 2 gm
Cal from fat 38%
Chol 0 mg
Sodium 88 mg

2 cups unbleached all-purpose flour
1 cup whole-wheat flour
2 teaspoons baking powder
1/2 teaspoon salt
1 teaspoon ground cinnamon
1/2 teaspoon ground mace
1 cup maple syrup granules or brown sugar

1 cup fructose or table sugar (sucrose)
2/3 cup vegetable oil
3/4 cup unsweetened applesauce
2/3 cup mashed tofu
3 cups peeled, diced Granny Smith apples
2/3 cup walnuts, chopped

Preheat oven to 350F (175C). Spray 2 (9 × 5-inch) loaf pans with vegetable oil spray. In a small bowl, stir together flours, baking powder, salt, cinnamon, and mace; set aside.

In a large bowl, beat together maple syrup granules, fructose, oil, applesauce, and tofu with an electric mixer until smooth. Add flour mixture to applesauce mixture and beat until combined. Stir in apples and walnuts.

Pour batter into prepared loaf pans and bake 1 hour or until a wooden pick inserted into the centers comes out clean. Cool in pans 10 minutes. Turn breads out onto a wire rack to finish cooling. Cut into slices.

ORANGE-CRANBERRY BREAD

Makes 2 loaves; 20 slices

The combination of sweet succulent orange and tart cranberries makes for a palate-pleasing contrast.

4 cups unbleached all-purpose flour
2 teaspoons baking powder
2 teaspoons baking soda
1 teaspoon salt
1 cup butter, softened
2 cups fructose or table sugar (sucrose)

1 cup egg whites or liquid egg substitute
2 cups plain nonfat yogurt
1/2 cup canned whole cranberry sauce
2 tablespoons freshly grated orange rind
1/4 cup freshly squeezed orange juice
3 tablespoons orange extract

Preheat oven to 350F (165C). Spray 2 (9 × 5-inch) loaf pans with vegetable oil spray. Into a small bowl, sift together flour, baking powder, baking soda, and salt; set aside.

In a medium bowl, beat together butter and fructose until smooth. Add egg whites and yogurt and beat until thoroughly combined. Add flour mixture, cranberry sauce, orange rind, and orange extract to yogurt mixture and beat until combined.

Pour batter into prepared pans. Bake 50 or 60 minutes or until a wooden pick inserted into the centers comes out clean. Cool in pans 10 minutes. Turn breads out onto a wire rack to finish cooling. Cut into slices.

BANANA-TOFU BREAD

Makes 2 loaves; 20 slices

You'll never detect the tofu that replaces the eggs in this great-tasting bread.
Using tofu reduces cholesterol considerably in this easy-to-make recipe.

2 3/4 cups unbleached all-purpose flour
2 teaspoons baking soda
3/4 cup butter or margarine, softened
1 1/2 cups fructose or table sugar (sucrose)

1/2 cup mashed tofu
2 1/2 cups mashed ripe bananas
1/2 cup nonfat plain yogurt
1 teaspoon pure vanilla extract

PER SLICE
Cal 230
Carb 7 gm
Prot 3 gm
Total fat 7 gm
Sat fat 4 gm
Cal from fat 27%
Chol 18 mg
Sodium 157 mg

Preheat oven to 350F (175C). Spray 2 (9 × 5-inch) loaf pans with vegetable oil spray. Into a small bowl, sift together flour and baking soda; set aside.

In a large bowl, beat butter and fructose with an electric mixer until light and creamy. Add tofu, bananas, yogurt, and vanilla and beat until smooth. Add flour mixture to banana mixture and beat until combined, about 1 minute.

Pour batter into prepared pans. Bake about 60 minutes or until a wooden pick inserted into the centers comes out clean. Cool in pans 10 minutes. Turn breads out onto a wire rack to finish cooling. Cut into slices.

BEST PUMPKIN BREAD

Makes 1 loaf; 10 slices

This wonderful recipe was given to me by two very dear people, Nina and Richard of Gourmet Coffee Warehouse in Venice, California. I went absolutely crazy over this bread the first time I tried it! Pumpkin bread has never tasted quite like this.

1 2/3 cups unbleached all-purpose flour
1 teaspoon baking soda
1/4 teaspoon salt
1/2 teaspoon ground cinnamon
1/2 teaspoon nutmeg
1 1/4 cups fructose or table sugar (sucrose)

1/3 cup vegetable oil
1/2 cup egg whites or liquid egg substitute
1/3 cup apple juice
1 1/4 cups canned pumpkin
1/2 cup pecans (optional), chopped

Preheat oven to 350F (175C). Spray a 9 × 5-inch loaf pan with vegetable oil spray. In a small bowl, sift together flour, baking soda, salt, cinnamon, and nutmeg; set aside.

In a large bowl, beat fructose, oil, egg whites, apple juice, and pumpkin with an electric mixer until light and creamy, about 1 minute. Add flour mixture and pecans to pumpkin mixture and stir until thoroughly combined.

Pour into prepared loaf pan. Bake 60 minutes or until a wooden pick inserted in center comes out clean. Cool in pan 10 minutes. Turn bread out onto a wire rack to finish cooling. Cut into slices.

BANANA BREAD

Makes 3 large loaves; 30 slices

Nonfat yogurt and mashed bananas make this a supermoist, flavorful bread. I give this to friends around the holidays and it's always a hit. I can't tell you how many times I've heard, "This is the best banana bread I've ever had."

3 1/4 cups unbleached all-purpose flour
2 teaspoons baking soda
3/4 cup butter, softened
1 1/2 cups fructose or table sugar (sucrose)

3 cups mashed ripe bananas
1 cup egg whites or liquid egg substitute
3/4 cup nonfat plain yogurt

Preheat oven to 350F (175C). Spray 3 (9 × 5-inch) loaf pans with vegetable oil spray. Into a small bowl, sift together flour and baking soda; set aside.

In a large bowl, beat butter and fructose with an electric mixer until light and creamy, about 2 minutes. Add bananas, egg whites, and yogurt and beat until smooth. Add flour mixture to banana mixture and mix until thoroughly blended, about 1 minute.

Pour into prepared loaf pans. Bake 60 minutes or until a wooden pick inserted in centers comes out clean. Cool in pans 10 minutes. Turn breads out onto a wire rack to finish cooling. Cut into slices.

DAIRY-FREE STRAWBERRY-BLUEBERRY BREAD

Makes 2 loaves; 20 slices

PER SLICE
Cal 256
Carb 41 gm
Prot 4 gm
Total fat 9 gm
Sat fat 1 gm
Cal from fat 32%
Chol 0 mg
Sodium 64 mg

Very berry, moist, and delicious strawberry-blueberry bread—berry lovers will be pleased indeed.

3 cups unbleached all-purpose flour
1 teaspoon baking soda
2 teaspoons ground cinnamon
2 1/2 cups fresh strawberries, mashed, or
   2 (10-oz.) packages frozen strawberries,
   thawed

1 cup liquid egg substitute or egg whites
2 cups fructose or table sugar (sucrose)
3/4 cup canola oil
3/4 cup fresh blueberries

Preheat oven to 350F (175C). Spray 2 (9 × 5-inch) loaf pans with vegetable oil spray. Into a small bowl, sift together flour, baking soda, and cinnamon.

In a medium bowl, beat strawberries, egg substitute, fructose, and oil with an electric mixer until thoroughly combined. Add strawberry mixture to flour mixture and mix to combine. Gently stir in blueberries.

Pour into prepared loaf pans. Bake 50 to 60 minutes or until a wooden pick inserted in centers comes out clean. Cool in pans 10 minutes. Turn breads out onto a wire rack to finish cooling. Cut into slices.

SWEET POTATO, CHUNKY APPLE, AND PECAN BREAD

Makes 2 loaves; 20 slices

Great for breakfast, this is a very hearty, wholesome, fiber-filled bread. The combination of sweet potato and dried apples, with pecans added for crunch and texture, makes this a winner any time of the day.

PER SLICE
Cal 159
Carb 23 gm
Prot 3 gm
Total fat 7 gm
Sat fat 0 gm
Cal from fat 39%
Chol 0 mg
Sodium 74 mg

1 cup whole-wheat flour
1 cup unbleached all-purpose flour
1 tablespoon baking powder
2 teaspoons pumpkin pie spice
1/4 cup unsweetened applesauce
1/3 cup safflower oil
1 cup maple syrup granules or
   granulated brown sugar

1/2 cup liquid egg substitute or egg whites
1 cup cooked, mashed sweet potato,
   fresh or canned
1 cup dried apples, chopped
3/4 cup pecans, chopped

Preheat oven to 350F (175C). Spray 2 (9 × 5-inch) loaf pans with vegetable oil spray. In a small bowl, stir together flours, baking powder, and spice; set aside.

In a large bowl, beat applesauce, oil, maple syrup granules, egg substitute, and sweet potato with an electric mixer until thoroughly blended. Add flour mixture to sweet potato mixture and beat until blended. Stir in dried apples and pecans.

Pour into prepared loaf pans. Bake 40 minutes or until a wooden pick inserted in centers comes out clean. Cool in pans 10 minutes. Turn breads out onto a wire rack to finish cooling. Cut into slices.

ZUCCHINI BREAD

Makes 2 loaves; 20 slices

PER SLICE
Cal 215
Carb 37 gm
Prot 3 gm
Total fat 6 gm
Sat fat 1 gm
Cal from fat 25%
Chol 0 mg
Sodium 232 mg

This excellent tea bread is full of flavor, spice, and crunch. It stays fresh and moist for almost a week and can even be kept frozen for up to three months. This is a favorite around the holidays.

2 1/2 cups unbleached all-purpose flour
2 teaspoons baking soda
1 teaspoon baking powder
1 1/2 teaspoons ground cinnamon
3/4 cup liquid egg substitute or
　egg whites

1/2 cup canola oil
1/2 cup canned pumpkin
2 cups fructose or table sugar (sucrose)
1 1/2 teaspoons pure vanilla extract
2 cups grated zucchini
1 cup pecans (optional), chopped

Preheat oven to 350F (175C). Spray 2 (9 × 5-inch) loaf pans with vegetable oil spray. Into a small bowl, sift together flour, baking soda, baking powder, and cinnamon; set aside.

In a large bowl, beat egg substitute, oil, pumpkin, fructose, and vanilla until combined. Fold in zucchini and pecans. Add zucchini mixture to flour mixture and beat until combined.

Pour into prepared loaf pans. Bake 70 minutes or until a wooden pick inserted in center comes out clean. Cool in pans 10 minutes. Turn breads out onto a wire rack to finish cooling. Cut into slices.

NONFAT CINNAMON-RAISIN ROLLS

Makes 18 rolls

These moist, juicy buns contain no butter, oil, or shortening. They are, in my opinion, just as good as the ones full of fat. For variation, use peaches or raspberry jam in place of raisins.

PER ROLL
Cal 257
Carb 56 gm
Prot 6 gm
Total fat 0.5 gm
Sat fat 0 gm
Cal from fat 0%
Chol 0 mg
Sodium 30 mg

DOUGH
2 tablespoons active dry yeast
1/2 cup warm water
1/2 cup nonfat (skim) milk, warmed
1/2 cup fructose or table sugar (sucrose)
1/2 cup liquid egg substitute or egg whites
1/2 cup plain nonfat yogurt
5 cups unbleached all-purpose flour

FILLING
2 tablespoons unsweetened applesauce
1 1/2 teaspoons ground cinnamon
3 tablespoons maple syrup granules or
   granulated brown sugar
1 cup raisins

GLAZE
1 cup fructose or table sugar (sucrose)
1 cup nonfat (skim) milk

Make dough: In a large bowl, dissolve yeast in warm water. Let stand until foamy, about 5 minutes. Add milk, fructose, egg substitute, yogurt, and 2 1/2 cups of the flour. Beat with an electric mixer until smooth. Add remaining flour and mix with your hands to make a soft dough.

Turn out dough onto a lightly floured board. Knead about 5 minutes or until smooth. Place in a large bowl sprayed with vegetable oil spray. Cover and let rise until doubled in size, about 1 1/2 hours.

While dough is rising, make filling: Combine all filling ingredients in a small bowl. Spray a baking sheet with vegetable oil spray.

Turn out dough onto floured board, knead lightly, and cut dough into 2 equal pieces. Roll out half of dough to about 1/4-inch thickness. Spread with half of the filling, roll up jelly-roll style, and pinch ends to seal. Cut into 9 slices, each about 1 1/2 inches wide. Repeat with remaining dough and filling.

Arrange rolls, cut side down, on prepared baking sheet, about 2 inches apart. Cover with an oiled piece of plastic wrap and let rise until doubled in size, about 1 hour.

Preheat oven to 375F (190C). Bake rolls 25 minutes or until browned. Prepare glaze while rolls are baking: Combine fructose and milk in a small bowl. Brush glaze on rolls as soon as they come out of the oven. Serve warm.

BEVERLY HILLS
MACADAMIA STICKY BUNS

Makes 12 rolls

The only fat in our buns are the macadamia nuts. That's because they are made without butter, oil, or egg yolks. These beautiful, bodacious buns will leave you breathless!

PER ROLL
Cal 233
Carb 102 gm
Prot 9 gm
Total fat 12 gm
Sat fat 2 gm
Cal from fat 20%
Chol 0 mg
Sodium 94 mg

DOUGH
2 packages active dry yeast
1/4 cup warm water
3/4 cup nonfat (skim) milk, warmed
1 tablespoon pumpkin pie spice
1 cup maple syrup granules or
    granulated brown sugar
1/2 cup nonfat plain yogurt
1/2 cup liquid egg substitute
4 1/2 cups unbleached all-purpose flour

FILLING
3/4 cup peach puree (1/2 cup peaches and
    1/4 cup peach juice blended together)
1/4 cup maple syrup granules or
    granulated brown sugar
2 teaspoons ground cinnamon
3/4 cup chopped peaches
1/2 cup golden raisins
2/3 cup macadamia nuts, chopped

TOPPING
2 cups pure maple syrup
2/3 cup macadamia nuts, chopped

Make dough: In a large bowl, dissolve yeast in warm water. Add warm milk, spice, maple syrup granules, yogurt, and egg substitute; mix well. Beat in enough flour to make a soft dough.

Knead dough on a floured board 2 minutes or until smooth. Transfer to a large bowl that has been sprayed with vegetable oil spray. Cover and let dough rise until doubled in size, about 2 hours.

While dough is rising, prepare filling: In a small bowl, combine all filling ingredients. Spray a large baking pan with vegetable oil spray.

Turn out dough onto a floured surface and roll out to a 1/4-inch-thick rectangle. Spread with the filling. Roll dough up like a jelly roll and pinch the ends to seal in filling. Cut dough crosswise into 12 slices, each about 1 inch wide.

Prepare topping: In a small bowl, combine maple syrup and nuts and spread evenly on the bottom of prepared baking pan. Place rolls, cut side down, on top of topping. Cover with an oiled piece of plastic wrap and let rise until doubled in size, about 1 hour.

Preheat oven to 350F (175C). Bake rolls 30 to 40 minutes or until golden in color. Remove from oven, invert onto a large plate, and serve warm.

DROP COOKIES, BAR COOKIES, BROWNIES, AND BISCOTTI

Nothing warms the heart more than homemade cookies or brownies fresh out of the oven, served with a glass of ice-cold milk. I still find this to be one of life's simplest and greatest pleasures.

Nostalgic memories of my childhood include Grandma Ethyl's kitchen and the home-baked cookies she made daily during my summer visits. It was in her kitchen that my future career began. I mastered the art of cookie baking by age ten, and to this day it remains my specialty.

Included in this very special chapter are a number of delicious nonfat bars and low-fat cookies. (The twice-baked biscotti are sensational and a popular treat that goes well with coffee.) Many of the recipes, however, are old family favorites, which means they did not fit into the category of low fat but they did fit the category of delectable!

With all my desserts, I generally try to find ways to cut fat and sugar wherever possible, but with cookies, especially rolled and drop cookies, it's more difficult. Ingredients such as reduced-fat margarine, reduced-fat peanut butter, and egg whites instead of yolks help reduce the fat. Cutting down on the amount of chocolate chips and nuts is another way to make cookies lower in fat and calories.

Even though we are primarily a healthy bakery, focusing on cutting down on fat and calories in our products, we do make some "traditional" cookies. In fact, we send hundreds of freshly baked, warm traditional cookies to Brentwood mansions on a daily basis.

Baking Tip

I recommend using an ice cream scoop for dropping the cookie dough onto the baking sheets to give cookies a professional look that is uniform in shape and size. Ice cream scoops are available in several different sizes at kitchen supply stores.

THE MILLION-DOLLAR PEANUT BUTTER CRUNCH COOKIE

Makes 30 cookies

This is the most divine peanut butter cookie I have ever tasted. You will not be disappointed with this "one of the great ones" recipe.

PER COOKIE
Cal 132
Carb 22 gm
Prot 3 gm
Total fat 4 gm
Sat fat 1 gm
Cal from fat 25%
Chol 0 mg
Sodium 116 mg

1/2 cup reduced-fat margarine
1/2 cup creamy reduced-fat peanut butter
1 1/2 cups maple syrup granules or
   granulated brown sugar
1/2 cup fructose or table sugar (sucrose)
4 egg whites

2 cups unbleached all-purpose flour
1 teaspoon baking soda
1/2 teaspoon baking powder
1 cup quick-cooking rolled oats
2 cups Special K cereal
1/3 cup sweetened flaked coconut

Preheat oven to 325F (175C). In a large bowl, beat margarine, peanut butter, maple syrup granules, fructose, and egg whites until creamy.

Into a medium bowl, sift together flour, baking soda, and baking powder; stir into creamed mixture. Add oats, cereal, and coconut and stir until combined.

Using an ice cream scoop, drop the dough in mounds about 1 inch apart onto ungreased baking sheets. Bake 20 minutes or until golden brown. Cool slightly on baking sheet, then remove to a wire rack to cool completely.

LOW-FAT OATMEAL-RAISIN COOKIES

Makes 30 cookies

PER COOKIE
Cal 76
Carb 16 gm
Prot 1 gm
Total fat 1 gm
Sat fat 0 gm
Cal from fat 12%
Chol 2 mg
Sodium 72 mg

*My long journey to create the ultimate crisp, low-fat cookie is finally over.
I found that most low-fat cookies tend to be soft and very cakelike.
These incredible buttery, lightly spiced, crispy cookies are best served warm
with ice-cold milk.*

1 cup unbleached all-purpose flour
1 teaspoon baking powder
1/2 teaspoon baking soda
1/2 teaspoon salt
2 tablespoons butter or margarine, melted
1/4 cup unsweetened applesauce
2/3 cup fructose or table sugar (sucrose)

1/3 cup maple syrup granules or
    granulated brown sugar
1/4 cup egg whites or liquid egg substitute
1 1/2 teaspoons pure vanilla extract
1 1/3 cups rolled oats
1/2 cup golden raisins
1/4 cup dark raisins

Preheat oven to 375F (190C). Spray a baking sheet with vegetable oil spray. Into a small bowl, sift together flour, baking powder, baking soda, and salt; set aside. In a large bowl, whisk butter, applesauce, fructose, maple syrup granules, egg whites, and vanilla. Add flour mixture to applesauce mixture and stir until thoroughly combined. Fold in oats and raisins.

Drop by rounded teaspoonfuls about 1 inch apart onto prepared baking sheet. Bake 10 to 12 minutes or until lightly browned. Cool slightly on baking sheet, then remove to a wire rack to cool completely.

CHUNKY CHOCOLATE
OATMEAL COOKIES

Makes about 40 cookies

These best-selling cookies are perfectly suited for royalty. They are unbelievably decadent, while being one of the simplest recipes to prepare.

PER COOKIE
Cal 92
Carb 14 gm
Prot 2 gm
Total fat 3 gm
Sat fat 1 gm
Cal from fat 29%
Chol 7 mg
Sodium 86 mg

1 3/4 cups unbleached all-purpose flour
1 teaspoon baking powder
1 teaspoon baking soda
1/2 teaspoon salt
1/2 cup butter, softened
2/3 cup fructose or table sugar (sucrose)
3/4 cup maple syrup granules or
    granulated brown sugar

1/2 cup egg whites or liquid egg substitute
1 teaspoon pure vanilla extract
1 1/2 cups quick-cooking rolled oats
1/2 cup chocolate chips
1/2 cup chopped milk chocolate bar

Preheat oven to 375F (190C). Into a small bowl, sift together flour, baking powder, baking soda, and salt; set aside. In a large bowl, beat butter and sugars with an electric mixer until light and creamy. Add egg whites and vanilla; beat until smooth. Add flour mixture to butter mixture and stir until thoroughly blended. Stir in oats and chocolate.

Drop by teaspoonfuls about 1 inch apart onto an ungreased baking sheet. Bake 12 to 15 minutes or until set. Cool slightly on baking sheet, then remove to a wire rack to cool completely.

PINEAPPLE, COCONUT, MACADAMIA NUT COOKIES

Makes 24 cookies

PER COOKIE
Cal 231
Carb 35 gm
Prot 3 gm
Total fat 9 gm
Sat fat 2 gm
Cal from fat 35%
Chol 0 mg
Sodium 113 mg

If you are looking for paradise, look no further. The combination of pineapple juice, coconut, and macadamias will send your taste buds to a tropical oasis.

2 1/2 cups unbleached all-purpose flour
1 teaspoon baking soda
1/2 teaspoon salt
1/2 cup vegetable oil
3/4 cup egg whites or liquid egg substitute
1 3/4 cups fructose or table sugar (sucrose)
1/4 cup maple syrup granules or
   granulated brown sugar

3/4 cup crushed canned pineapple,
   undrained
1 cup quick-cooking rolled oats
2 cups corn flakes
3/4 cup flaked coconut
3/4 cup macadamia nuts, chopped

Preheat oven to 350F (175C). Spray a baking sheet with vegetable oil spray. Into a small bowl, sift together flour, baking soda, and salt; set aside.

In a large bowl, beat oil, egg whites, fructose, maple syrup granules, and pineapple with an electric mixer until thoroughly combined. Add flour mixture to pineapple mixture and stir until combined. Stir in oats, corn flakes, coconut, and macadamia nuts; mix until incorporated.

Drop by teaspoonfuls about 1 inch apart onto prepared baking sheet. Bake 20 minutes or until golden. Cool slightly on baking sheet, then remove to a wire rack to cool completely.

DOUBLE PEANUT BUTTER
AND CORNMEAL
COOKIES

Makes 18 cookies

This recipe is very simple to prepare: it can be made in one bowl. Cornmeal adds a wonderful crunchy texture. The combination of chocolate and peanut butter chips makes these cookies absolutely seductive.

PER COOKIE
Cal 193
Carb 27 gm
Prot 6 gm
Total fat 7 gm
Sat fat 2 gm
Cal from fat 32%
Chol 0 mg
Sodium 189 mg

1 1/4 cups unbleached all-purpose flour
3/4 cup yellow cornmeal
1/2 teaspoon baking powder
1/4 teaspoon salt
3/4 cup fructose or table sugar (sucrose)

2 tablespoons vegetable oil
1/2 cup egg whites or liquid egg substitute
3/4 cup reduced-fat peanut butter
1/2 cup peanut butter chips
1/2 cup chocolate chips (optional)

Preheat oven to 350F (175C). Spray a baking sheet with vegetable oil spray. In a large bowl, stir together flour, cornmeal, baking powder, salt, and fructose. Add oil, egg whites, and peanut butter; whisk until thoroughly combined. Stir in peanut butter chips and chocolate chips.

Drop by teaspoonfuls about 1 inch apart onto prepared baking sheet. Bake 20 minutes or until lightly browned. Cool slightly on baking sheet, then remove to a wire rack to cool completely.

NONFAT RAISIN CLOUD COOKIES

Makes 12 cookies

PER COOKIE
Cal 110
Carb 28 gm
Prot 1 gm
Total fat 0 gm
Sat fat 0 gm
Cal from fat 0%
Chol 0 mg
Sodium 33 mg

This recipe was given to me by my in-laws, Andy and Genie Holmberg. I never dreamed these meringue cookies would turn out to be one of my favorites. Very simple to prepare, they need to be made the day before serving: the secret to their light texture is leaving them in the oven overnight. Serve with ice cold milk.

2 egg whites
2/3 cup fructose or table sugar (sucrose)

1/8 teaspoon salt
1 1/2 cups raisins

Preheat oven to 350F (175C). Spray a baking sheet with vegetable oil spray. In a medium bowl, beat egg whites, sugar, and salt with an electric mixer until stiff peaks form. Stir in raisins.

Drop by teaspoonfuls about 1 inch apart onto prepared baking sheet. Place cookies in oven, turn off oven heat, and leave in oven 8 hours. Remove from oven and remove from baking sheet.

VARIATION
Add 1/2 cup chocolate chips with raisins.

LOW-FAT
CARROT-CAKE
COOKIES

Makes 24 cookies

A welcome addition to our low-fat collection. Customers simply adore the taste of carrot cake in a cookie. You can have your cake and eat it too!

PER COOKIE
Cal 88
Carb 18 gm
Prot 2 gm
Total fat 1 gm
Sat fat 0 gm
Cal from fat 13%
Chol 2 mg
Sodium 91 mg

3/4 cup unbleached all-purpose flour
1/4 cup whole-wheat pastry flour
1 teaspoon baking powder
1/2 teaspoon baking soda
1/2 teaspoon ground cinnamon
1/2 teaspoon salt
2 tablespoons butter or margarine, melted
1/4 cup baby-food carrots
1/2 cup fructose or table sugar (sucrose)

1/2 cup maple syrup granules or
    granulated brown sugar
1/4 cup egg whites or liquid egg substitute
1 teaspoon pure vanilla extract
1 1/3 cups rolled oats
1/2 cup raisins
1/4 cup crushed fresh or
    canned pineapple, drained

Preheat oven to 375F (190C). Spray a baking sheet with vegetable oil spray. In a small bowl, stir together flours, baking powder, baking soda, cinnamon, and salt; set aside.

In a large bowl, beat butter, carrots, fructose, maple syrup granules, egg whites, and vanilla with an electric mixer until thoroughly combined. Add flour mixture to carrot mixture and beat until incorporated. Stir in oats, raisins, and pineapple; mix well.

Drop by teaspoonfuls about 1 inch apart onto prepared baking sheet. Bake 10 to 12 minutes or until lightly browned. Cool slightly on baking sheet, then remove to a wire rack to cool completely.

TRIPLE-CHOCOLATE BLISS COOKIES

Makes 24 cookies

PER COOKIE
Cal 99
Carb 16 gm
Prot 1 gm
Total fat 3 gm
Sat fat 1 gm
Cal from fat 27%
Chol 0 mg
Sodium 95 mg

If this isn't chocolate bliss, I don't know what is. White chocolate chips and milk chocolate chunks in a most satisfying and glorious chocolate-based cookie.

1 1/2 cups unbleached all-purpose flour
1/2 cup unsweetened cocoa powder
1/2 teaspoon baking soda
1/4 teaspoon salt
1/2 cup reduced-fat margarine
2/3 cup fructose or table sugar (sucrose)
1/3 cup maple syrup granules or
   granulated brown sugar

1/4 cup egg whites or liquid egg substitute
1/4 cup strong coffee
1 teaspoon pure vanilla extract
1/3 cup white chocolate chips
1/2 cup chopped milk chocolate bar

Preheat oven to 325F (165C). Spray a baking sheet with vegetable oil spray. Into a small bowl, sift together flour, cocoa, baking soda, and salt; set aside. In a large bowl, beat butter, fructose, and maple syrup granules with an electric mixer until light and creamy. Add egg whites and beat until thoroughly combined. Add flour mixture, coffee, and vanilla to chocolate mixture and stir until incorporated. Fold in white chocolate chips and milk chocolate bar.

Drop by teaspoonfuls about 1 inch apart onto prepared baking sheet. Bake 15 to 20 minutes. Cool slightly on baking sheet, then remove to a wire rack to cool completely.

LEMON-VANILLA CHIP COOKIES

Makes 38 cookies

Vanilla chips are indeed the perfect partner for these irresistibly crispy lemon cookies. If vanilla chips are not available to you, white chocolate chips will work as well.

PER COOKIE
Cal 110
Carb 18 gm
Prot 1 gm
Total fat 3 gm
Sat fat 2 gm
Cal from fat 29%
Chol 7 mg
Sodium 83 mg

2 1/2 cups unbleached all-purpose flour
1 teaspoon baking soda
1/2 teaspoon salt
1/2 cup butter, softened
1 1/2 cups fructose or table sugar (sucrose)

1/2 cup egg whites
1 tablespoon freshly squeezed lemon juice
2 tablespoons fresh lemon rind
2 teaspoons lemon extract
3/4 cup vanilla or white chocolate chips

Preheat oven to 350F (175C). Spray a baking sheet with vegetable oil spray. Into a small bowl, sift together flour, baking soda, and salt; set aside. In a large bowl, beat butter and sugar with an electric mixer until light and creamy. Add egg whites, lemon juice, lemon rind, and lemon extract. Mix until thoroughly combined. Add flour mixture to butter mixture and stir until incorporated. Fold in vanilla chips.

Drop by teaspoonfuls about 1 inch apart onto prepared baking sheet. Bake 12 to 15 minutes or until lightly browned. Cool slightly on baking sheet, then remove to a wire rack to cool completely.

BUTTERSCOTCH CHIP COOKIES

Makes 36 cookies

PER COOKIE
Cal 123
Carb 17 gm
Prot 2 gm
Total fat 5 gm
Sat fat 3 gm
Cal from fat 36%
Chol 7 mg
Sodium 79 mg

My husband and son love the taste of butterscotch. I can never bake enough of these. My guys eat them faster than I make them. Save some cookie dough to top your favorite frozen dessert. Butterscotch-cookie-dough ice cream is a big hit in my home.

2 1/2 cups unbleached all-purpose flour

1/2 teaspoon baking soda

1 teaspoon ground cinnamon

1/2 cup butter, softened

3/4 cup fructose or table sugar (sucrose)

3/4 cup maple syrup granules or granulated brown sugar

1/2 cup egg whites or liquid egg substitute

1 teaspoon pure vanilla extract

1/2 cup butterscotch chips

1/2 cup vanilla or white chocolate chips

1/2 cup walnuts, chopped

Preheat oven to 350F (175C). Into a small bowl, sift together flour, baking soda, and cinnamon; set aside. In a large bowl, beat butter, fructose, maple syrup granules, egg whites, and vanilla until light and creamy. Add flour mixture to butter mixture and beat until incorporated. Stir in butterscotch chips, vanilla chips, and walnuts.

Drop by teaspoonfuls about 1 inch apart onto ungreased baking sheet. Bake 15 minutes or until lightly browned. Cool slightly on baking sheet, then remove to a wire rack to cool completely.

PUMPKIN-SPICE COOKIES

Makes 24 cookies

Pumpkin spice and everything nice are what these cookies are made of. My children love to have me make these for Santa Claus every Christmas Eve.

PER COOKIE
Cal 115
Carb 19 gm
Prot 1 gm
Total fat 4 gm
Sat fat 2 gm
Cal from fat 31%
Chol 10 mg
Sodium 132 mg

2 cups unbleached all-purpose flour
1 teaspoon baking soda
1 teaspoon baking powder
1/2 teaspoon salt
1 teaspoon ground cinnamon
1/2 teaspoon ground nutmeg
1/2 cup butter or margarine, softened

3/4 cup fructose or table sugar (sucrose)
1/4 cup maple syrup granules or
   granulated brown sugar
1 cup canned pumpkin
1/2 cup golden raisins
1/2 cup walnuts (optional), chopped

Preheat oven to 350F (175C). Spray a baking sheet with vegetable oil spray. Into a small bowl, sift together flour, baking soda, baking powder, salt, cinnamon, and nutmeg; set aside. In a large bowl, beat butter, fructose, maple syrup granules, and pumpkin with an electric mixer until light and creamy. Add flour mixture to pumpkin mixture and beat until incorporated. Stir in raisins and nuts.

Drop by teaspoonfuls about 1 inch apart onto prepared baking sheet. Bake 15 to 20 minutes or until lightly browned. Cool slightly on baking sheet, then remove to a wire rack to cool completely.

WHOLE-WHEAT
SNICKER DOODLES

Makes about 36 cookies

These cookies are great for kids and adults alike. The addition of whole-wheat flour creates a healthier treat so you can feel good about giving them to your family.

PER COOKIE
Cal 106
Carb 19 gm
Prot 1 gm
Total fat 3 gm
Sat fat 2 gm
Cal from fat 22%
Chol 7 mg
Sodium 85 mg

1 3/4 cups unbleached all-purpose flour
1 cup whole-wheat flour
2 teaspoons cream of tartar
1 teaspoon baking soda
1/2 teaspoon salt
1/2 cup butter or margarine, softened
1 1/2 cups fructose or table sugar (sucrose)
1/2 cup egg whites or liquid egg substitute

CINNAMON SUGAR
1/4 cup fructose or table sugar (sucrose)
1 tablespoon ground cinnamon

Preheat oven to 350F (175C). In a small bowl, stir together flours, cream of tartar, baking soda, and salt; set aside. In a large bowl, beat butter, fructose, and egg whites with an electric mixer until light and creamy. Add flour mixture to butter mixture and beat until thoroughly combined. Wrap dough in plastic wrap and chill in refrigerator 60 minutes.

Make cinnamon sugar: In a small bowl, combine fructose and cinnamon. Roll dough into 2-inch balls, dust with cinnamon-sugar, and place about 1 inch apart on an ungreased baking sheet. Bake 10 to 15 minutes or until lightly browned. Cool slightly on baking sheet, then remove to a wire rack to cool completely.

L.A.'S BEST
CHOCOLATE CHIP
COOKIES

Makes 24 cookies

The customers at Krystine's Healthy Gourmet Bakery in Brentwood came up with the name for these cookies. A best-seller and they are fabulous! Pure maple syrup granules and high-quality chocolate make them, in my opinion, the best cookies in the world!

PER COOKIE
Cal 147
Carb 20 gm
Prot 2 gm
Total fat 6 gm
Sat fat 3 gm
Cal from fat 36%
Chol 10 mg
Sodium 106 mg

2 cups unbleached all-purpose flour
1 teaspoon baking soda
1/2 cup butter, softened
1/4 cup reduced-fat margarine
1 1/2 cups maple syrup granules or
    3/4 cup fructose
    and 3/4 cup granulated brown sugar

1/2 cup egg whites
1 teaspoon pure vanilla extract
1/2 cup rolled oats, ground fine in a
    blender or food processor
3/4 cup chocolate chips

Preheat oven to 325F (160C). Spray a baking sheet with vegetable oil spray. Into a small bowl, sift together flour and baking soda; set aside. In a large bowl, beat butter, margarine, and maple granules with an electric mixer until smooth. Add egg whites and vanilla and beat 15 seconds. Add flour mixture to butter mixture and stir until thoroughly combined. Stir in ground oats and chocolate chips.

Using an ice cream scoop, drop the batter in mounds about 1 inch apart onto prepared baking sheet. Bake 12 to 15 minutes. Cool slightly on baking sheet, then remove to a wire rack to cool completely.

OATMEAL, VANILLA CHIP, MACADAMIA COOKIES

Makes 30 cookies

PER COOKIE
Cal 144
Carb 17 gm
Prot 2 gm
Total fat 7 gm
Sat fat 2 gm
Cal from fat 43%
Chol 7 mg
Sodium 130 mg

These cookies are "totally awesome!" My mother calls them the world's best cookies. They are her very favorite. Though not fat free, these small wonders are worth every gram of fat. The combination of macadamia nuts and vanilla chips makes them truly magnificent.

1 cup reduced-fat margarine	1 teaspoon baking soda
1 1/2 cups maple syrup granules or	1/2 teaspoon baking powder
3/4 cup fructose	1 cup rolled oats
and 3/4 cup granulated brown sugar	1 1/2 cups corn flakes, crushed
1 egg	1/2 cup sweetened flaked coconut,
1/4 cup liquid egg substitute	chopped
1 teaspoon pure vanilla extract	3/4 cup macadamia nuts
2 cups unbleached all-purpose flour	3/4 cup vanilla or white chocolate chips

Preheat oven to 350F (175C). In a small bowl, beat margarine, maple syrup granules, egg, egg substitute, and vanilla with an electric mixer until combined. Into another small bowl, sift together flour, baking soda, and baking powder. Add flour mixture to butter mixture and beat until smooth. Stir in oats, corn flakes, coconut, nuts, and vanilla chips.

Drop batter by teaspoonfuls about 1 inch apart onto ungreased baking sheet. Bake 15 minutes. Cool slightly on baking sheet, then remove to a wire rack to cool completely.

WHEAT-FREE, DAIRY-FREE, PEANUT BUTTER COOKIES

Makes 12 cookies

These crispy, nutty, flourless, dairy-free cookies can be made in a snap. They're a winner in my home and will be in yours, too!

2 cups reduced-fat peanut butter
2 cups fructose or table sugar (sucrose)
2 teaspoons pure vanilla extract
1/2 cup liquid egg substitute or egg whites
3/4 cup peanuts, chopped

Preheat oven to 325F (160C). Spray a baking sheet with vegetable oil spray. In a large bowl, beat peanut butter, fructose, vanilla, and egg substitute with an electric mixer until light and creamy. Stir in chopped peanuts.

Using an ice cream scoop, drop batter in mounds about 2 inches apart onto ungreased baking sheet. Smash cookies down with floured bottom of a drinking glass. Bake 15 to 25 minutes or until lightly browned. Cool slightly on baking sheet, then remove to a wire rack to cool completely.

BLUE-RIBBON
FUDGY BROWNIES

Makes 18 brownies

PER BROWNIE
WITHOUT
FROSTING
Cal 205
Carb 32 gm
Prot 3 gm
Total fat 8 gm
Sat fat 1 gm
Cal from fat 34%
Chol 23 mg
Sodium 143 mg

This award-winning recipe has been in my family for decades. I have altered the original recipe so that the fat and cholesterol have been reduced considerably. All of the ingredients can be prepared in one pan. It's as easy as one, two, three! Thank you, Aunt Jan, for this sensational recipe.

1 cup reduced-fat margarine
1/2 cup unsweetened cocoa powder
2 eggs
1/2 cup egg whites or liquid egg substitute
2 cups fructose or table sugar (sucrose)

3/4 cup unbleached all-purpose flour
1/2 cup walnuts, chopped
1 teaspoon pure vanilla extract
Chocolate Walnut Icing (page 169),
  optional

Preheat oven to 400F (205C). Spray a 15 × 10-inch baking pan with cooking oil spray. In a large saucepan, melt margarine with cocoa over low heat. Remove from heat. Whisk in eggs, egg whites, fructose, and flour until thoroughly combined. Stir in walnuts and vanilla.

Pour into prepared baking pan. Bake 25 to 30 minutes. Cool in pan on a wire rack. Frost with icing, if desired. Cut into 18 pieces.

CHOCOLATE-RASPBERRY
CHEESECAKE BROWNIES

Makes 12 brownies

Low-fat raspberry cream cheese heightens the taste of chocolate most pleasantly. Gooey and rich, these chocolate raspberry delights are sure to please.

PER BROWNIE
Cal 264
Carb 47 gm
Prot 6 gm
Total fat 6 gm
Sat fat 0 gm
Cal from fat 20%
Chol 7 mg
Sodium 154 mg

1 cup unbleached all-purpose flour
3/4 cup unsweetened cocoa powder
2/3 cup reduced-fat margarine
1 1/2 cups fructose or table sugar (sucrose)
1 cup liquid egg substitute
1 teaspoon pure vanilla extract

TOPPING
1 (8-ounce) package light cream cheese, softened
1/2 cup chocolate chips
1/3 cup fruit-sweetened raspberry preserves

Preheat oven to 350F (175C). Spray an 8-inch-square baking pan with vegetable oil spray. Into a medium bowl, sift together flour and cocoa. Add margarine and fructose and beat until thoroughly combined. Gradually whisk in egg substitute, then vanilla.

Pour into prepared pan. Make topping: In a medium bowl, beat together all topping ingredients with an electric mixer until thoroughly combined. Drop rounded teaspoonfuls of topping onto brownie batter. Bake 35 to 45 minutes. Cool in pan on a wire rack. Cut into 12 bars.

CHOCOLATE-TOFU FUDGE BROWNIES

Makes 12 brownies

PER BROWNIE
Cal 360
Carb 52 gm
Prot 5 gm
Total fat 15 gm
Sat fat 5 gm
Cal from fat 37%
Chol 20 mg
Sodium 108 mg

A very simple egg-free recipe that is made in one pan. Don't let the tofu scare you because these are just as rich and fabulous as traditional brownies.

1/2 cup butter or margarine
2/3 cup unsweetened cocoa powder
1 cup mashed tofu
2 cups fructose or table sugar (sucrose)

1 1/4 cups unbleached all-purpose flour
1 teaspoon baking powder
1 cup walnuts, chopped
1 teaspoon pure vanilla extract

Preheat oven to 375F (190C). Spray an 8-inch-square baking pan with vegetable oil spray. In a medium saucepan, melt butter with cocoa. Remove from heat and whisk in, one at a time, tofu, fructose, flour, baking powder, walnuts, and vanilla, mixing well after each addition.

Spread batter in prepared baking pan. Bake 30 to 40 minutes or until a wooden pick inserted in center comes out clean. Cool in pan on a wire rack. Cut brownies into 12 rectangles.

CAPPUCCINO-MALT BROWNIES

Makes 12 brownies

These treats were inspired by my infatuation with coffee malted milkshakes. I serve them to my dinner guests with generous scoops of espresso ice cream.

PER BAR
Cal 332
Carb 47 gm
Prot 6 gm
Total fat 15 gm
Sat fat 5 gm
Cal from fat 41%
Chol 23 mg
Sodium 157 mg

1 1/3 cups unbleached all-purpose flour
1 teaspoon baking powder
1/2 cup butter or margarine
1/4 cup unsweetened cocoa powder
1 1/2 cups chocolate chips

1 cup egg whites or liquid egg substitute
1 cup fructose or table sugar (sucrose)
3/4 cup malted milk powder
2 teaspoons very strong coffee
1 teaspoon pure vanilla extract

Preheat oven to 325F (165C). Spray an 8-inch-square baking pan with vegetable oil spray. Into a small bowl, sift together flour and baking powder; set aside. In a medium saucepan, melt butter, cocoa, and chocolate chips over low heat, stirring occasionally. Remove from heat and whisk in egg whites, fructose, malted milk powder, coffee, and vanilla, mixing well after each addition. Add flour mixture and stir until thoroughly incorporated.

Spread batter in prepared baking pan. Bake 40 minutes. Cool in pan on a wire rack. Cut into 12 bars.

BUTTERSCOTCH BROWNIES

Makes 18 brownies

A great alternative for those who don't indulge in chocolate, these blonde bars are as rich and buttery as a fudge brownie. Their distinctive taste comes from a mouthful of butterscotch chips in every bite.

2 cups unbleached all-purpose flour
1 1/2 teaspoons baking powder
1/2 teaspoon salt
3/4 cup reduced-fat margarine
1 2/3 cups maple syrup granules or
   granulated brown sugar

1 cup egg whites or liquid egg substitute
2 1/2 teaspoons pure vanilla extract
1 cup butterscotch chips

Preheat oven to 350F (175C). Spray a 13 × 9-inch baking pan with vegetable oil spray. Into a small bowl, sift together flour, baking powder, and salt; set aside. In a large saucepan, melt margarine over low heat. Remove from heat and stir in maple syrup granules, egg whites, flour mixture, and vanilla, mixing well after each addition. Stir in butterscotch chips.

Pour batter in prepared pan. Bake 30 minutes. Cool in pan on a wire rack. Cut into 18 bars.

BANANA-MOCHA BUTTERSCOTCH BROWNIES

Makes 12 bars

An essential for your brownie collection, these bars have a moist texture that comes from fresh ripe bananas. Coffee and butterscotch chips intensify the flavor and make them simply magnificent.

PER BROWNIE
Cal 380
Carb 65 gm
Prot 5 gm
Total fat 12 gm
Sat fat 6 gm
Cal from fat 28%
Chol 21 mg
Sodium 122 mg

1/2 cup butter or margarine	1 1/2 cups unbleached all-purpose flour
2 tablespoons unsweetened cocoa powder	1 teaspoon pure vanilla extract
3/4 cup mashed ripe bananas	1/4 cup strong coffee
1 cup egg whites or liquid egg substitute	1/2 cup chocolate chips
2 cups fructose or table sugar (sucrose)	1/2 cup butterscotch chips

Preheat oven to 375F (190C). Spray an 8-inch-square pan with vegetable oil spray. In a medium saucepan, melt butter with cocoa over low heat. Remove from heat and stir in bananas, egg whites, fructose, flour, vanilla, coffee, and chips until incorporated.

Spread batter in prepared pan. Bake 15 minutes. Cool in pan on a wire rack. Cut into 12 bars.

NONFAT BROWNIES

Makes 12 brownies

PER BROWNIE
Cal 75
Carb 16 gm
Prot 2 gm
Total fat 0 gm
Sat fat 0 gm
Cal from fat 0%
Chol 0 mg
Sodium 13 mg

These chewy and moist brownies are a great alternative to the traditional recipe. Prunes replace the butter and make them delectable.

2/3 cup baby-food prunes
1/3 cup egg whites or liquid egg substitute
1/2 cup unsweetened cocoa powder

1/2 cup fructose or table sugar (sucrose)
1/2 cup unbleached all-purpose flour

Preheat oven to 400F (205C). Spray an 8-inch-square baking pan with vegetable oil spray. In a medium bowl, combine prunes, egg whites, cocoa, fructose, and flour. Whisk until combined.

Spread batter in prepared pan. Bake 20 minutes or until a wooden pick inserted into center comes out clean. Cool in pan on a wire rack. Cut into 12 bars.

DAIRY-FREE
FRESH APPLE BARS

Makes 15 bars

Fuji apples make these cakelike bars scrumptious. There are no butter or milk products added for those of you concerned with lactose. My son loves to eat these for breakfast, and I feel good giving them to him.

PER BAR
Cal 148
Carb 16 gm
Prot 3 gm
Total fat 8 gm
Sat fat 1 gm
Cal from fat 48%
Chol 0 mg
Sodium 77 mg

3/4 cup liquid egg substitute or egg whites
3/4 cup canola oil
1/4 cup unsweetened applesauce
1 1/2 cups maple syrup granules or table
  sugar (sucrose), plus 1/3 cup for sprinkling

2 cups unbleached all-purpose flour
1 teaspoon baking soda
1/2 teaspoon ground cinnamon
2 cups peeled, finely chopped Fuji apples
1 cup walnuts (optional), chopped

Preheat oven to 350F (175C). Spray a 13 × 9-inch baking pan with vegetable oil spray. In a large bowl, beat egg substitute, oil, applesauce, and 1 1/2 cups maple syrup granules with an electric mixer until light and fluffy; set aside. Into a small bowl, sift together flour, baking soda, and cinnamon. Add flour mixture to applesauce mixture and stir until combined. Stir in apples and walnuts.

Pour into prepared pan. Bake 30 to 40 minutes. Sprinkle with maple syrup granules. Cool in pan on a wire rack. Cut into 15 bars.

NONFAT PEACH-HAZELNUT BARS

Makes 12 bars

PER BAR
Cal 274
Carb 58 gm
Prot 6 gm
Total fat 0 gm
Sat fat 0 gm
Cal from fat 0%
Chol 0 mg
Sodium 141 mg

First let me say these peach bars are phenomenal! Second, I must give credit to Paula Amemiya for giving me this wonderful gift. These are supermoist little cakes with just a hint of hazelnut and loads of fresh peaches. You're gonna love them.

Topping (see opposite)
1/2 cup unsweetened applesauce
1 1/2 cups fructose or table sugar (sucrose)
1/4 cup hazelnut extract
1 cup liquid egg substitute
2 cups unbleached all-purpose flour
1 teaspoon baking soda
1 teaspoon baking powder
1/2 teaspoon ground nutmeg
3/4 cup sour milk [3/4 cup nonfat (skim) milk mixed with 1 tablespoon apple cider vinegar]
1/4 cup maple syrup granules

TOPPING
2 large ripe peaches, peeled and cut into slices
1/4 cup fructose or table sugar (sucrose)
1/4 cup unbleached all-purpose flour
1/4 teaspoon ground nutmeg
1/4 teaspoon ground cinnamon

Preheat oven to 350F (175C). Spray an 8-inch-square baking pan with vegetable oil spray. Make topping: In a small bowl, gently toss peaches, fructose, flour, nutmeg, and cinnamon. Arrange peach slices on bottom of pan; set aside.

In a large bowl, beat applesauce, sugar, and hazelnut extract with an electric mixer until combined. Add egg substitute, 1/3 cup at a time, beating well after each addition. Into a small bowl, sift together flour, baking soda, baking powder, and nutmeg. Stir flour mixture into applesauce mixture, alternately with sour milk. Beat 1 minute.

Pour into prepared pan. Bake 50 minutes. Let cool in pan 45 minutes, then turn upside down on a serving dish. Sprinkle with maple syrup granules while still warm.

APRICOT-OATMEAL BARS

Makes 12 bars

Great to stuff into lunch boxes or take these wholesome-tasting and satisfying treats along on family outings. I love the addition of vanilla chips, which enhance the apricots quite nicely.

PER BAR
Cal 353
Carb 62 gm
Prot 2 gm
Total fat 11 gm
Sat fat 7 gm
Cal from fat 28%
Chol 21 mg
Sodium 93 mg

1 cup rolled oats
1/2 cup unbleached all-purpose flour
1 cup maple syrup granules or
   granulated brown sugar

1/2 cup butter, chilled
1 3/4 cups apricot preserves
1/2 cup dried apricots, diced
3/4 cup vanilla or white chocolate chips

Preheat oven to 350F (175C). Spray an 8-inch-square baking pan with vegetable oil spray. Mix oats, flour, maple syrup granules, and butter with a pastry blender until crumbly.

Place one-half of the mixture in prepared pan and pat down to make bottom crust. Cover with apricot preserves, dried apricots, and vanilla chips. Top with remaining oat mixture.

Bake 40 minutes or until lightly browned. Cool in pan on a wire rack. Cut into 12 bars.

CRANBERRY-BUTTERSCOTCH
TOFU SQUARES

Makes 16 squares

PER BAR
Cal 277
Carb 53 gm
Prot 3 gm
Total fat 6 gm
Sat fat 2 gm
Cal from fat 21%
Chol 0 mg
Sodium 198 mg

This recipe was given to me by Cathy Morgan, the mother of one of my son's friends. I replaced the eggs in the original recipe with tofu—no one will ever know the difference. The unusual combination of butterscotch and cranberries makes these bars uniquely satisfying. My husband loves taking them to work. Their dense texture makes them great for traveling or shipping to faraway places.

2 cups unbleached all-purpose flour	2 cups fructose or table sugar (sucrose)
1 teaspoon baking powder	2/3 cup mashed tofu
1/2 teaspoon salt	1 cup dried cranberries
3/4 cup reduced-fat margarine	1/2 cup butterscotch chips

Preheat oven to 350F (175C). Spray an 8-inch-square pan with vegetable oil spray. Into a small bowl, sift together flour, baking powder, and salt; set aside.

In a large bowl, beat margarine, fructose, and tofu with an electric mixer until light and creamy. Add flour mixture to butter mixture and beat until well blended. Fold in cranberries and butterscotch chips.

Press mixture into prepared pan. Bake 30 to 40 minutes or until golden brown. Cool in pan on a wire rack. Cut into 16 squares.

VARIATION
Use chopped fresh cranberries if dried ones are not available.

WHOLE-WHEAT CHOCOLATE ZUCCHINI BARS

Makes 24 bars

I'm constantly looking for creative ways to sneak in vegetables for my children. They love these chocolate bars and cannot detect the zucchini in them. Made with whole-wheat flour and topped with the optional maple pecan frosting, they look as luscious as they taste!

PER BAR
WITHOUT
FROSTING
Cal 203
Carb 29 gm
Prot 3 gm
Total fat 10 gm
Sat fat 3 gm
Cal from fat 44%
Chol 15 mg
Sodium 158 mg

1 cup unbleached all-purpose flour
1 cup whole-wheat pastry flour
1/4 cup unsweetened cocoa powder
1 teaspoon ground cinnamon
1 teaspoon baking soda
1/2 teaspoon salt
3/4 cup butter, softened
1 cup fructose or table sugar (sucrose)
1 cup maple syrup granules or
   granulated brown sugar

1 cup egg whites or liquid egg substitute
3 ounces unsweetened chocolate, melted
1/2 cup sour milk [1 1/2 teaspoons
   vinegar combined with 1/2 cup nonfat
   (skim) milk]
3/4 cup very hot water
2 cups shredded zucchini
1 cup chocolate chips
Maple Coconut-Pecan Frosting
   (page 166) (optional)

Preheat oven to 350F (175C). Spray a 13 × 9-inch baking pan with vegetable oil spray. In a small bowl, stir together flours, cocoa, cinnamon, baking soda, and salt; set aside.

In a large bowl, beat butter, fructose, maple syrup granules, and egg whites with an electric mixer until light and creamy. Add melted chocolate, sour milk, and hot water. Beat until thoroughly incorporated. Add flour mixture to chocolate mixture and stir until combined. Stir in zucchini and chocolate chips.

Spread batter in prepared baking pan. Bake 30 minutes or until a wooden pick inserted in center comes out clean. Cool in pan on a wire rack. Top with frosting. Cut into 24 bars.

OATMEAL SCOTCH SQUARES

Makes 16 squares

"Devilishly delicious" comes to mind after taking one bite out of these sinfully rich butterscotch bars.

PER SQUARE
Cal 208
Carb 28 gm
Prot 3 gm
Total fat 10 gm
Sat fat 5 gm
Cal from fat 43%
Chol 15 mg
Sodium 95 mg

1 cup unbleached all-purpose flour
3/4 cup whole-wheat pastry flour
1 teaspoon baking powder
1/2 cup butter, softened
1/2 cup unsweetened applesauce
1/2 cup fructose or table sugar (sucrose)
1/2 cup maple syrup granules or
  granulated brown sugar

1/4 cup egg whites or liquid egg
  substitute
1 teaspoon pure vanilla extract
1/2 cup butterscotch chips
1/2 cup chopped walnuts
1 egg white, for brushing
1/2 cup rolled oats

Preheat oven to 325F (165C). In a small bowl, stir together flours and baking powder; set aside. In a medium bowl, beat butter, applesauce, fructose, maple syrup granules, the 1/4 cup egg whites, and vanilla with an electric mixer until light and creamy. Add flour mixture to butter mixture and beat until combined. Stir in butterscotch chips and nuts.

Spread dough in an ungreased 8-inch-square baking pan and pat into an even layer. Brush with 1 egg white and sprinkle with rolled oats. Bake 30 to 35 minutes or until golden brown. Cool in pan on a wire rack. Cut into 16 bars.

CHOCOLATE CHIP–DATE BARS

Makes 24 bars

This recipe has been in my family for years, handed down from one generation to the next. The original recipe calls for 2 cups of butter. I've cut the fat, but they taste just as rich and sinful as the originals.

2 1/2 cups unbleached all-purpose flour
1 teaspoon baking soda
2/3 cup reduced-fat margarine
1/3 cup baby-food carrots
1 cup egg whites or liquid egg substitute
1 cup maple syrup granules or
   granulated brown sugar

1 cup fructose or table sugar (sucrose)
1 cup quick-cooking rolled oats
2 teaspoons pure vanilla extract
1 cup dates, chopped
1/2 cup chocolate chips

PER BAR
Cal 188
Carb 35 gm
Prot 3 gm
Total fat 4 gm
Sat fat 0 gm
Cal from fat 19%
Chol 0 mg
Sodium 116 mg

Preheat oven to 325F (165C). Into a small bowl, sift together flour and baking soda; set aside. In a medium bowl, beat margarine, carrots, egg whites, maple syrup granules, fructose, oats, and vanilla with an electric mixer until light and creamy. Add flour mixture and stir until thoroughly combined. Stir in dates and chocolate chips.

Spread batter in an ungreased 8-inch-square baking pan. Bake 30 to 35 minutes or until golden brown. Cool in pan on a wire rack. Cut into 24 bars.

CHOCOLATE-APRICOT SQUARES

Makes 16 squares

Dried apricots and milk chocolate add a delightful contrast. Applesauce is used to reduce the fat content. This bar travels well and can be kept in the refrigerator up to ten days.

1/2 cup unbleached all-purpose flour
1/3 cup whole-wheat flour
1/2 teaspoon baking soda
1/4 cup egg whites or liquid egg substitute
1/4 cup vegetable oil
2 tablespoons unsweetened applesauce
1/2 cup fructose or table sugar (sucrose)

1/4 cup maple syrup granules or
   granulated brown sugar
1 teaspoon pure vanilla extract
1/4 cup rolled oats
1/2 cup dried apricots, chopped
3/4 cup chopped milk chocolate bar
1/2 cup pecans, chopped

Preheat oven to 350F (175C). Spray an 8-inch-square baking pan with vegetable oil spray. In a small bowl, stir together flours and baking soda; set aside. In a large bowl, beat egg whites, oil, applesauce, fructose, maple syrup granules, and vanilla with an electric mixer until thoroughly combined. Add flour mixture to applesauce mixture and beat until incorporated. Stir in oats, apricots, milk chocolate, and pecans.

Spread batter in prepared pan and bake 30 minutes or until lightly browned. Cool in pan on a wire rack. Cut into 16 squares.

LEMON CHOCOLATE SHORTBREAD

Makes 20 servings

This flaky, buttery English chocolate shortbread, lightly scented with fresh lemon rind, can be made in one bowl. It's a lovely complement to hot Earl Grey tea.

PER SERVING
Cal 101
Carb 15 gm
Prot 1 gm
Total fat 3 gm
Sat fat 1 gm
Cal from fat 31%
Chol 0 mg
Sodium 83 mg

3/4 cup reduced-fat margarine
1/2 cup fructose or table sugar (sucrose)
2 teaspoons lemon extract

2 tablespoons grated lemon rind
2 cups unbleached all-purpose flour
1/3 cup unsweetened cocoa powder

Preheat oven to 350F (175C). In a large bowl, beat margarine, fructose, lemon extract, and lemon rind with an electric mixer until light and creamy. Stir in flour and cocoa and mix until thoroughly combined.

Divide dough into 2 equal balls. Press one ball into a 9-inch pie pan. Repeat with remaining dough. Cut dough in each pan into 10 wedges. Bake 20 minutes or until lightly browned. Cool in pan on a wire rack.

CHOCOLATE-RASPBERRY STREUSEL SQUARES

Makes 16 bars

PER BAR
Cal 286
Carb 49 gm
Prot 3 gm
Total fat 9 gm
Sat fat 2 gm
Cal from fat 28%
Chol 0 mg
Sodium 167 mg

This easy-to-make recipe was given to me by a super mom and terrific lady, Cathy Morgan. The white and chocolate chips enhance the flavor of the raspberry preserves. These streusel bars are completely egg free. They make a great snack to be enjoyed any time of the day. Thank you, Cathy, for a superb recipe.

1 1/2 cups unbleached all-purpose flour
1 teaspoon baking powder
1/4 teaspoon salt
1 1/2 cups rolled oats
1/2 cup fructose or table sugar (sucrose)
1/2 cup maple syrup granules or
   granulated brown sugar

3/4 cup reduced-fat margarine, chilled
1 cup raspberry preserves
3/4 cup vanilla or white chocolate chips
3/4 cup chocolate chips

Preheat oven to 375F (190C). In a large bowl, combine flour, baking powder, salt, oats, fructose, and maple syrup granules. Cut in margarine with a pastry blender until mixture is well blended and crumbly. Reserve 1 cup oat mixture for topping; set aside.

Press remaining oat mixture onto bottom of an ungreased 8-inch-square baking pan. Bake 10 minutes; remove from oven. Spread preserves over crust; sprinkle evenly with topping, then vanilla and chocolate chips, patting gently. Bake 30 minutes or until golden brown. Cool in pan on a wire rack. Cut into 16 squares.

LOW-FAT
SUN-KISSED
ORANGE BISCOTTI

Makes 28 cookies

These cookies are a refreshing treat. With the added touch of orange, they can be served at any occasion.

PER COOKIE
Cal 80
Carb 16 gm
Prot 2 gm
Total fat 0.5 gm
Sat fat 0 gm
Cal from fat 5%
Chol 22 mg
Sodium 52 mg

2 1/4 cups unbleached all-purpose flour
1 cup fructose or table sugar (sucrose)
1 teaspoon baking powder
1/2 teaspoon baking soda
1/4 teaspoon salt
3 large eggs

1 teaspoon pure vanilla extract
2 1/2 tablespoons freshly grated
   orange rind
2 tablespoons freshly squeezed
   orange juice

Preheat oven to 325F (165C). Spray a large baking sheet with vegetable oil spray. Into a large bowl, sift together flour, fructose, baking powder, baking soda, and salt; set aside. In a small bowl, beat eggs, vanilla, orange rind, and orange juice with an electric mixer until thoroughly combined. Add orange juice mixture to flour mixture and beat until well blended.

Using floured hands, form dough into 2 (12-inch-long) strips; flatten to 1-inch thickness. Arrange logs on prepared baking sheet. Bake 25 minutes or until firm to the touch.

Remove rolls from baking sheet to a wire rack; let cool 10 minutes. Reduce oven temperature to 275F (135C). Using a serrated knife, cut logs diagonally into 1/2-inch-thick slices. Arrange slices, cut side down, on baking sheet. Bake 30 minutes. Transfer cookies to a wire rack and cool completely.

PISTACHIO-CRANBERRY BISCOTTI

Makes 28 cookies

The vibrant colors of red cranberries and green pistachios give this no-butter-added cookie the appearance of the holidays without all the fat.

PER COOKIE
Cal 110
Carb 19 gm
Prot 3 gm
Total fat 3 gm
Sat fat 0 gm
Cal from fat 24%
Chol 22 mg
Sodium 74 mg

2 cups unbleached all-purpose flour
3/4 cup fructose or table sugar (sucrose)
1 teaspoon baking powder
1/2 teaspoon baking soda
1/2 teaspoon salt
3 eggs

1 egg white
2 teaspoons pure vanilla extract
1 tablespoon freshly squeezed orange
  juice
1 cup dried cranberries
1 cup chopped pistachios

Preheat oven to 325F (165C). Spray a large baking sheet with vegetable oil spray. Into a large bowl, sift together flour, fructose, baking powder, baking soda, and salt; set aside. In a small bowl, beat eggs, egg white, vanilla, and orange juice with an electric mixer until thoroughly combined. Add egg mixture to flour mixture and beat until well blended. Stir in cranberries and pistachios.

Using floured hands, form dough into 2 (12-inch-long) strips; flatten to 1-inch thickness. Arrange logs on prepared baking sheet. Bake 25 minutes or until firm to the touch.

Remove rolls from baking sheet to a wire rack; let cool 10 minutes. Reduce oven temperature to 275F (135C). Using a serrated knife, cut logs diagonally into 1/2-inch-thick slices. Arrange slices, cut side down, on baking sheet. Bake 30 minutes. Transfer cookies to a wire rack and cool completely.

WHOLE WHEAT-PEANUT BUTTER BISCOTTI

Makes 28 cookies

Whole-wheat flour and crunchy peanuts are a delicious and healthy combination.

1 cup whole-wheat flour
1 cup unbleached all-purpose flour
1 cup fructose or table sugar (sucrose)
1 teaspoon baking powder
1/2 teaspoon baking soda
1/4 teaspoon salt

1/2 cup reduced-fat creamy peanut butter
2 large eggs
2 egg whites
1 teaspoon pure vanilla extract
1/2 cup peanuts, chopped

PER COOKIE
Cal 131
Carb 18 gm
Prot 4 gm
Total fat 5 gm
Sat fat 1 gm
Cal from fat 34%
Chol 15 mg
Sodium 82 mg

Preheat oven to 325F (165C). Spray a large baking sheet with vegetable oil spray. In a large bowl, stir together flours, fructose, baking powder, baking soda, and salt; set aside. In a small bowl, beat peanut butter, eggs, egg whites, and vanilla with an electric mixer until thoroughly combined. Add peanut butter mixture to flour mixture and beat until well blended. Stir in peanuts.

Using floured hands, form dough into 2 (12-inch-long) strips; flatten to 1-inch thickness. Arrange logs on prepared baking sheet. Bake 25 minutes or until firm to the touch.

Remove rolls from baking sheet to a wire rack; let cool 10 minutes. Reduce oven temperature to 275F (135C). Using a serrated knife, cut logs diagonally into 1/2-inch-thick slices. Arrange slices, cut side down, on baking sheet. Bake 30 minutes. Transfer cookies to a wire rack and cool completely.

LOW-FAT GINGERBREAD BISCOTTI

Makes 28 cookies

PER COOKIE
Cal 102
Carb 23 gm
Prot 2 gm
Total fat 1 gm
Sat fat 0 gm
Cal from fat 8%
Chol 15 mg
Sodium 55 mg

Cinnamon, spice, and everything nice are what these low-fat twice-baked cookies are made of.

2 cups unbleached all-purpose flour
1 cup fructose or table sugar (sucrose)
1 teaspoon baking powder
1/2 teaspoon baking soda
1/4 teaspoon salt
2 tablespoons ground cinnamon
2 teaspoons ground ginger

2 teaspoons ground nutmeg
2 large eggs
2 egg whites
2 tablespoons apple juice concentrate
1 teaspoon pure vanilla extract
1 1/2 cups raisins

Preheat oven to 325F (165C). Spray a large baking sheet with vegetable oil spray. Into a large bowl, sift together flour, fructose, baking powder, baking soda, salt, cinnamon, ginger, and nutmeg; set aside. In a small bowl, beat eggs, egg whites, apple juice concentrate, and vanilla with an electric mixer until thoroughly combined. Add egg mixture to flour mixture and beat until well blended. Stir in raisins.

Using floured hands, form dough into 2 (12-inch-long) strips; flatten to 1-inch thickness. Arrange logs on prepared baking sheet. Bake 25 minutes or until firm to the touch.

Remove rolls from baking sheet to a wire rack; let cool 10 minutes. Reduce oven temperature to 275F (135C). Using a serrated knife, cut logs diagonally into 1/2-inch-thick slices. Arrange slices, cut side down, on baking sheet. Bake 30 minutes. Transfer cookies to a wire rack and cool completely.

DARK AND WHITE CHOCOLATE-MACADAMIA BISCOTTI

Makes 28 cookies

This inviting combination may make you feel like you sinned after just one bite, but don't worry; there's no confessing with these no-added-butter cookies.

PER COOKIE
Cal 137
Carb 19 gm
Prot 2 gm
Total fat 5 gm
Sat fat 1 gm
Cal from fat 33%
Chol 23 mg
Sodium 59 mg

2 cups unbleached all-purpose flour
1/2 cup unsweetened cocoa powder
1 cup fructose or table sugar (sucrose)
1 teaspoon baking powder
1/2 teaspoon baking soda
1/4 teaspoon salt
3 eggs

2 egg whites
2 teaspoons pure vanilla extract
1 tablespoon strong coffee
3/4 cup macadamia nuts, chopped
1/2 cup vanilla or white chocolate chips
1/2 cup chocolate chips

Preheat oven to 325F(165C). Spray a large baking sheet with vegetable oil spray. Into a large bowl, sift together flour, cocoa, fructose, baking powder, baking soda, and salt; set aside. In a small bowl, beat eggs, egg whites, vanilla, and coffee with an electric mixer until thoroughly combined. Add egg mixture to flour mixture and beat until well blended. Stir in macadamia nuts, vanilla chips, and chocolate chips.

Using floured hands, form dough into 2 (12-inch-long) strips; flatten to 1-inch thickness. Arrange logs on prepared baking sheet. Bake 25 minutes or until firm to the touch.

Remove rolls from baking sheet to a wire rack; let cool 10 minutes. Reduce oven temperature to 275F (135C). Using a serrated knife, cut logs diagonally into 1/2-inch-thick slices. Arrange slices, cut side down, on baking sheet. Bake 30 minutes. Transfer cookies to a wire rack and cool completely.

JEANETTE'S
ALMOND COOKIES

Makes 24 cookies

PER COOKIE
Cal 120
Carb 19 gm
Prot 3 gm
Total fat 4 gm
Sat fat 1 gm
Cal from fat 27%
Chol 0 mg
Sodium 82 mg

My editor (Jeanette Egan, whose undying passion for almonds—they are high in calcium) inspired me to come up with this sensational recipe.

2 cups unbleached all-purpose flour
1/2 teaspoon baking soda
1/2 teaspoon cream of tartar
1/2 cup reduced-fat margarine
1 cup fructose or table sugar (sucrose)
1/2 cup liquid egg substitute

1 tablespoon fresh lemon juice
2 teaspoons almond extract
1/2 cup slivered blanched almonds,
    chopped
1 teaspooon freshly grated lemon rind

Preheat oven to 350F (175C). Spray a baking sheet with vegetable oil spray. In a small bowl, sift together flour, baking powder, and cream of tartar.

In a large bowl, beat margarine, fructose, egg substitute, lemon juice, and almond extract with an electric mixer until light and creamy. Add flour mixture to butter mixture and stir until thoroughly incorporated. Fold in almonds and lemon rind.

Drop by teaspoonfuls onto prepared baking sheet. Bake 10 minutes, then flatten with a spatula. Bake an additional 5 to 7 minutes or until browned. Cool slightly on baking sheet, then remove to a wire rack to cool completely. Let cool at least 1 hour before serving; the cookies will become crisp as they cool.

this possible by using ingredients such as low-fat evaporated milk, nonfat milk, egg whites, and cocoa instead of chocolate. Even with these nonfat techniques the pies are still delicious. Good luck.

The crusts listed in the pie and tart recipes are only suggestions; you can mix and match them to suit your taste.

Baking Tip

When making your crusts it is important to remember not to overmix or overbeat once you add water to the flour mixture. This can make your crust soggy, unworkable, and just plain undesirable.

PIES AND TARTS

Historically, eating pies has been regarded as one of America's favorite pastimes. Pies are much appreciated both as traditional winter holiday desserts and as simple summer delights. Being such a classic symbol, the pie is always a festive and grand way to make a room full of guests smile.

A lesser known cousin to the pie is the tart, a more elegant version of the pie that is generally made with custard, nuts, and fresh fruit of the season. It is versatile and can range in size. Also, it is a quick solution to a perfect dessert.

The pies and tarts are certainly the number one favorites at the bakery during the holiday season. Our first Christmas, the bakery had just opened two weeks prior and we were the only bakery in town to have a nonfat pumpkin pie filling. The patrons went nuts! Lines began forming out the door; everyone wanted one. I realized when the demand became greater than our supply, we were in trouble. Everyone I knew was called for help. My husband, a police officer, who has difficulty frying an egg, was called in. He in turn recruited his police-officer friends, who all showed up and became master pie makers in just a few hours. We were completely unprepared for the mass hysteria. I remember looking up at the baker's racks and seeing stacks of pies and pies and pies: it was absolute pie-mania! Of course now things are much more organized for whatever the holidays bring.

In this chapter you will find all my favorite recipes for pies and tarts. Each is unique not only in flavor but also in appearance. As you begin reviewing these you will discover a couple of recipes for nonfat crusts. Generally, however, it is difficult to reduce the fat of a basic pie crust without sacrificing taste, consistency, and quality. Instead, the fat reduction is done in the fillings. I have made

LIGHT LEMON-CHEESE PIE

Makes 1 pie; 10 servings

This reduced-fat pie has all the richness of a cream cheese pie with only half the fat.

1 1/2 cups light cream cheese, softened
1/2 cup liquid egg substitute
3/4 cup fructose or table sugar (sucrose)
1 teaspoon lemon extract
1 teaspoon freshly squeezed lemon juice
1 tablespoon freshly grated lemon rind
1 (9-inch) Graham Cracker Crust
    (page 109)

TOPPING
1 1/2 cups nonfat sour cream
1/4 cup fructose or table sugar (sucrose)
1 teaspoon pure vanilla extract

PER SERVING
Cal 288
Carb 33 gm
Prot 6 gm
Total fat 15 gm
Sat fat 5 gm
Cal from fat 47%
Chol 12 mg
Sodium 324 mg

Preheat oven to 350F (175C). In a medium bowl, beat cream cheese, egg substitute, fructose, lemon extract, lemon juice, and lemon rind with an electric mixer until smooth and creamy. Pour into prepared pie crust. Bake 20 minutes or until filling is set.

Cool 15 minutes. While pie is cooling, make topping: In a small bowl, blend sour cream, fructose, and vanilla until smooth. Spread on top of cheese pie and refrigerate 6 or more hours before serving.

SWEET POTATO PIE

Makes 1 pie; 10 servings

A great Thanksgiving alternative to the traditional pumpkin pie.

2 1/3 cups mashed, cooked sweet potatoes
1 cup fructose or table sugar (sucrose)
2/3 cup liquid egg substitute
1 1/4 cups low-fat evaporated milk
1 teaspoon pure vanilla extract

1 teaspoon ground cinnamon
1/2 teaspoon ground nutmeg
1 (9-inch) Standard Pie Crust (page 115),
    Whole-Wheat Pastry Crust (page 111),
    or other crust, unbaked

Preheat oven to 400F (205C). In a large bowl, combine all of the filling ingredients. Whisk thoroughly until smooth and creamy. Pour into prepared pie crust.

Bake 50 to 60 minutes or until a knife inserted off-center comes out clean. Serve warm or chilled.

LOW-FAT CUSTARD PIE

Makes 1 pie; 10 servings

Very light and refreshing, it tastes sinfully rich, but it isn't.
You'll be very pleased.

PER SERVING
Cal 203
Carb 30 gm
Prot 6 gm
Total fat 6 gm
Sat fat 3 gm
Cal from fat 26%
Chol 13 mg
Sodium 177 mg

1 3/4 cups nonfat (skim) milk
1 tablespoon butter
3/4 cup fructose or table sugar (sucrose)
1 1/4 cups liquid egg substitute

2 teaspoons pure vanilla extract
1 (9-inch) Standard Pie Crust (page 115)
  or other crust, partially baked
1 teaspoon ground nutmeg

Preheat oven to 375F (190C). In a large saucepan, heat milk, butter, and fructose over low heat until hot and butter melts; do not boil. Remove from heat. Whisk in egg substitute and vanilla. Pour into unbaked pie crust. Sprinkle nutmeg on top.

Bake 35 minutes or until filling is firm. Serve chilled.

STRAWBERRY-RHUBARB PIE

Makes 1 pie; 10 servings

The tangy combination of fresh rhubarb and strawberries gives this very popular pie some attitude. Top it off with some low-fat vanilla ice cream or frozen yogurt.

PER SERVING
Cal 227
Carb 46 gm
Prot 2 gm
Total fat 4 gm
Sat fat 2 gm
Cal from fat 16%
Chol 10 mg
Sodium 100 mg

4 cups 1/2-inch pieces rhubarb
2 cups fresh strawberries, sliced
1 tablespoon freshly grated orange rind
1/3 cup unbleached all-purpose flour

1 1/4 cups fructose or table sugar (sucrose)
1 (9-inch) Whole-Wheat Pastry Crust
 (page 111), Standard Pie Crust
 (page 115), or other crust, unbaked

Preheat oven to 400F (205C). In a large bowl, lightly toss together rhubarb, strawberries, and orange rind with flour and sugar. Spoon into prepared pie crust.

Bake 1 hour or until crust is lightly browned and filling is bubbly. Serve warm or at room temperature.

TRIPLE-BERRY STREUSEL PIE

Makes 1 pie; 10 servings

Ah! The fresh taste of berries—what a refreshing way to top a wonderful meal. Great for those summer outings.

PER SERVING
Cal 328
Carb 59 gm
Prot 3 gm
Total fat 9 gm
Sat fat 3 gm
Cal from fat 25%
Chol 11 mg
Sodium 210 mg

2 cups raspberries, fresh or frozen
1 cup blueberries, fresh or frozen
1 cup boysenberries (or blackberries), fresh
   or frozen
1 cup fructose or table sugar (sucrose)
1/4 cup cornstarch
1 (9-inch) Whole-Wheat Pastry Crust
   (page 111), Standard Pie Crust
   (page 115), or other crust, unbaked

STREUSEL TOPPING
1/2 cup reduced-fat margarine, chilled
1/2 cup unbleached all-purpose flour
1/3 cup rolled oats
1/3 cup fructose or table sugar (sucrose)

Preheat oven to 375F (190C). In a medium bowl, lightly toss raspberries, blueberries, and boysenberries with sugar and cornstarch. Pour into prepared pie crust.

Make topping: In a small bowl, combine all topping ingredients. Mix with a pastry blender or your fingers until crumbly. Sprinkle topping over berries.

Bake 50 to 55 minutes or until crust is lightly browned and filling is bubbly. Serve warm or at room temperature.

PUMPKIN-TOFU PIE

Makes 1 pie; 10 servings

A terrific way to enjoy pumpkin pie without any egg or dairy products. We sell these pies by the hundreds during the Thanksgiving and Christmas holidays. So simple to make, it can be mixed in one bowl.

PER SERVING
Cal 243
Carb 33 gm
Prot 6 gm
Total fat 10 gm
Sat fat 5 gm
Cal from fat 37%
Chol 21 mg
Sodium 252 mg

1 1/2 cups mashed tofu
2 cups canned pumpkin
1/2 cup fructose or table sugar (sucrose)
1/4 cup maple syrup granules or
    granulated brown sugar
1/4 teaspoon salt
1 teaspoon ground cinnamon

1/2 teaspoon ground nutmeg
1/2 teaspoon ground ginger
1/2 teaspoon ground allspice
2 teaspoons pure vanilla extract
1 (9-inch) Whole-Wheat Pastry Crust
    (page 111) or other crust, unbaked

Preheat oven to 375F (190C). In a large bowl, combine all filling ingredients and whisk until thoroughly incorporated. Pour into prepared pie crust.

Bake 55 to 60 minutes or until filling is firm. Serve chilled.

WHITE CHOCOLATE-
LEMON PIE

Makes 1 pie; 10 servings

This rich-tasting, satisfying pie is terrific. Your taste buds will not detect the tofu, but you'll feel better knowing it's in there.

PER SERVING
Cal 264
Carb 29 gm
Prot 7 gm
Total fat 15 gm
Sat fat 6 gm
Cal from fat 51%
Chol 11 mg
Sodium 139 mg

2 1/2 cups mashed extra-firm tofu
1/2 cup pure maple syrup
1 cup vanilla or white chocolate chips, melted
2 tablespoons vegetable oil

2 teaspoons pure lemon extract
2 tablespoons freshly grated lemon rind
1 (9-inch) Whole-Wheat Pastry Crust (page 111), Standard Pie Crust (page 115), or other crust, unbaked

Preheat oven to 350F (175C). In a food processor or blender, combine tofu, maple syrup, melted chips, oil, lemon extract, and lemon rind. Process until thoroughly combined. Pour into prepared pie crust.

Bake 1 hour or until filling is firm. Cool in refrigerator 2 hours before serving.

BANANA-COCONUT-TOFU CREAM PIE

Makes 1 pie; 10 servings

The exotic combination of bananas and coconut gives this pie a tropical feel.

2 tablespoons pure lemon juice
1 tablespoon water
1 envelope unflavored gelatin
2 cups mashed tofu
1 1/2 cups mashed ripe bananas
1/2 cup fructose or table sugar (sucrose)

3/4 cup sweetened flaked coconut
1 teaspoon pure vanilla extract
1 (9-inch) Standard Pie Crust (page 115),
    Whole-Wheat Pastry Crust (page 111),
    or other crust, baked

In a small saucepan, combine lemon juice, water, and gelatin. Whisk over low heat until gelatin is completely dissolved. Remove from heat and cool 10 minutes.

In a food processor or blender, combine gelatin mixture, tofu, bananas, fructose, coconut, and vanilla. Process until thoroughly incorporated. Pour into prepared pie crust. Cool in refrigerator until set, about 2 hours, before serving.

VARIATION
Add 1/2 cup roasted and diced macadamia nuts (see page 31) to filling before adding to pie crust.

CHOCOLATE TOFU PIE

Makes 1 pie; 10 servings

Chocolate disguises the tofu in this pie so it is undetectable. Its smooth and creamy texture makes it a favorite with our vegetarian clientele.

2 1/2 cups extra-firm tofu
1/2 cup pure maple syrup
1 cup chocolate chips, melted
2 tablespoons vegetable oil

1 teaspoon pure vanilla extract
1 (9-inch) Standard Pie Crust (page 115),
   Whole-Wheat Pastry Crust (page 111),
   or other crust, baked

PER SERVING
Cal 315
Carb 35 gm
Prot 12 gm
Total fat 16 gm
Sat fat 3 gm
Cal from fat 45%
Chol 9 mg
Sodium 114 mg

Preheat oven to 350F (175C). In a food processor or blender, combine all filling ingredients. Process until smooth and creamy. Pour into prepared crust. Cool in the refrigerator 2 hours before serving.

PUMPKIN-PECAN PIE

Makes 1 pie; 10 servings

Make this a holiday tradition at your house as it is at mine.

PER SERVING
Cal 304
Carb 46 gm
Prot 6 gm
Total fat 12 gm
Sat fat 3 gm
Cal from fat 35%
Chol 9 mg
Sodium 149 mg

1 cup liquid egg substitute
2 cups canned pumpkin
1/2 cup fructose or table sugar (sucrose)
1/2 cup maple syrup granules or
   granulated brown sugar
1/2 cup pure maple syrup

1/2 teaspoon ground cinnamon
1 teaspoon pure vanilla extract
1 cup chopped pecans
1 (9-inch) Standard Pie Crust (page 115),
   Whole-Wheat Pastry Crust (page 111),
   or other crust, baked

Preheat oven to 400F (205C). In a large bowl, mix together all filling ingredients until blended. Pour into prepared pie crust.

Bake 50 to 60 minutes or until filling is set. Serve warm or at room temperature.

BUTTERSCOTCH PUDDING TART

Makes 1 tart; 12 servings

This creamy pie will bring back memories of warm butterscotch pudding, but without the fat and cholesterol of the original.

PER SERVING
Cal 226
Carb 32 gm
Prot 4 gm
Total fat 9 gm
Sat fat 4 gm
Cal from fat 36%
Chol 8 mg
Sodium 209 mg

1/3 cup water
1 1/2 cups maple syrup granules or
   granulated brown sugar
3 tablespoons unbleached all-purpose flour
1 3/4 cups nonfat (skim) milk
1/2 cup butterscotch chips

1/2 cup reduced-fat margarine
1/2 cup liquid egg substitute
1 teaspoon pure vanilla extract
1 (10-inch) Standard Pie Crust
   (page 115), Flaky Tart Crust
   (page 112), or other crust, baked

In a large saucepan, combine water, maple syrup granules, and flour until smooth. Add milk, butterscotch chips, and margarine. Cook over medium heat, stirring constantly, until mixture thickens and comes to a boil, about 10 minutes.

Remove from heat. Stir some of hot mixture into egg substitute and return mixture to saucepan. Bring to a boil, stirring constantly. Remove from heat and stir in vanilla. Pour into prepared tart crust. Refrigerate until chilled before serving.

CHOCOLATE MERINGUE-MOCHA PIE

Makes 1 pie; 10 servings

PER SERVING
Cal 370
Carb 71 gm
Prot 6 gm
Total fat 6 gm
Sat fat 3 gm
Cal from fat 14%
Chol 76 mg
Sodium 156 mg

Made with nonfat milk instead of heavy cream and cocoa in place of chocolate bars, this reduced-fat pie is just as decadent as the traditional recipe. The addition of fresh coffee truly brings out the chocolate flavor.

1/2 cup unsweetened cocoa powder
1 cup fructose or table sugar (sucrose)
1/3 cup cornstarch
2 3/4 cups nonfat (skim) milk
1/4 cup strong coffee
3 egg yolks
2 teaspoons butter
1 teaspoon pure vanilla extract
1 (9-inch) Standard Pie Crust (page 115),
  Whole-Wheat Pastry Crust (page 111),
  or other crust, baked

CHOCOLATE MERINGUE
4 egg whites
1/4 teaspoon cream of tartar
1 1/4 cups fructose or table sugar
  (sucrose)
2 tablespoons unsweetened cocoa
  powder, sifted
1 tablespoon cornstarch

Into a large saucepan, sift together cocoa, fructose, and cornstarch. Gradually whisk in milk and coffee. Cook over medium heat, stirring constantly, until mixture thickens and comes to a boil, about 10 minutes. Boil 1 minute; remove from heat.

In a small bowl, beat egg yolks until thick and lemon-colored. Stir a little of the hot mixture into yolks and return mixture to saucepan. Cook over medium heat, stirring constantly, 2 minutes. Remove from heat and stir in butter and vanilla. Pour into prepared crust.

Preheat oven to 400F (205C). Make meringue: In a medium bowl, beat egg whites and cream of tartar with an electric mixer until soft peaks form. Gradually add 1 cup of the fructose and beat until stiff peaks form. Fold in remaining 1/4 cup fructose, cocoa, and cornstarch. Spread over filling, sealing to the edge of the crust. Bake 8 minutes or until lightly browned. Serve warm or chilled.

APPLE CRUNCH PIE

Makes 1 pie; 10 servings

A favorite classic with a wonderful oatmeal-crunch top. Using apple juice concentrate as the primary sweetener truly brings out the fresh apple taste. Nonfat vanilla frozen yogurt à la mode is a must for this all American treat.

PER SERVING
Cal 268
Carb 38 gm
Prot 3 gm
Total fat 12 gm
Sat fat 5 gm
Cal from fat 40%
Chol 21 mg
Sodium 138 mg

6 cups peeled, sliced Granny Smith apples
3 teaspoons unbleached all-purpose flour
2 teaspoons ground cinnamon
1/3 cup apple juice concentrate
2 tablespoons maple syrup granules or
  granulated brown sugar
1 (9-inch) Standard Pie Crust (page 115),
  Cornmeal Crust (page 110), or other
  crust, unbaked

TOPPING
1/2 cup unbleached all-purpose flour
1/4 cup maple syrup granules or
  granulated brown sugar
1/4 cup unsalted butter
1/2 cup rolled oats
1/2 teaspoon ground cinnamon
1/2 cup finely chopped pecans

Preheat oven to 375F (190C). In a medium saucepan, combine sliced apples, flour, cinnamon, apple juice concentrate, and maple syrup granules. Cook over medium heat 10 minutes, stirring gently. Pour into prepared pie crust.

Make topping: In a small bowl, mix topping ingredients together using a fork or pastry blender until crumbly. Sprinkle topping over apple filling. Bake 45 minutes or until topping is golden. Serve warm or at room temperature.

BANANA CREAM PIE

Makes 1 pie; 10 servings

PER SERVING
Cal 189
Carb 33 gm
Prot 5 gm
Total fat 4 gm
Sat fat 2 gm
Cal from fat 19%
Chol 10 mg
Sodium 135 mg

I simply adore custard cream pies! It is a weakness I have had since childhood. This recipe has nonfat filling so you can devour it with only half the guilt.

1/2 cup fructose or table sugar (sucrose)
1/4 cup cornstarch
1 teaspoon unbleached all-purpose flour
2 1/2 cups nonfat (skim) milk
1/3 cup egg substitute or egg whites

2 teaspoons pure vanilla extract
2 medium bananas, sliced into rounds
1 (9-inch) Standard Pie Crust (page 115),
    Whole-Wheat Pastry Crust (page 111),
    or other crust, baked

Preheat oven to 400F (205C). In a large saucepan, combine fructose, cornstarch, and flour and whisk until smooth. Stir in milk. Cook over medium heat, stirring constantly, until mixture boils and thickens, about 10 minutes. Remove from heat. Stir some of hot mixture into egg substitute and return mixture to saucepan. Cook, stirring constantly, until slightly thickened. Remove from heat and stir in vanilla and sliced bananas. Pour into prepared pie crust. Cool in the refrigerator 2 hours before serving.

NONFAT
LEMON MERINGUE
PIE

Makes 1 pie; 10 servings

A light, tangy lemon filling with a nonfat meringue crust. Very refreshing! Very delicious!

PER SERVING
Cal 214
Carb 48 gm
Prot 5 gm
Total fat 0 gm
Sat fat 0 gm
Cal from fat 0%
Chol 0 mg
Sodium 71 mg

1 cup fructose or table sugar (sucrose)
3 tablespoons cornstarch
1 cup boiling water
1/4 cup fresh lemon juice
1 teaspoon freshly grated lemon rind
1 1/4 cups egg whites or liquid egg
   substitute
1 (9-inch) Nonfat Meringue Crust
   (page 114), baked

MERINGUE
3 egg whites
2 tablespoons fructose or table sugar
   (sucrose)

Preheat oven to 375F (190C). In a medium saucepan, whisk together fructose, cornstarch, and boiling water. Cook over low heat, stirring constantly, until thick and smooth. Remove from heat and stir in lemon juice, lemon rind, and egg whites. Cook 2 to 3 minutes, stirring constantly. Pour into baked meringue shell.

Make meringue: In a large bowl, beat egg whites and fructose until stiff peaks form. Spread over filling, sealing to the edge of the crust. Bake 15 minutes or until light brown. Serve chilled.

PECAN PIE

Makes 2 (9-inch) pies; 20 servings

PER SERVING
Cal 292
Carb 32 gm
Prot 5 gm
Total fat 17 gm
Sat fat 4 gm
Cal from fat 52%
Chol 15 mg
Sodium 153 mg

This pecan pie filling is so sinfully rich you won't believe it only has four ingredients. How can something so simple be that good? Try it and see.

1 1/2 cups liquid egg substitute
2 cups maple syrup granules or
   granulated brown sugar or
   1 1/2 cups pure maple syrup

4 tablespoons butter, softened
3 cups pecan halves
2 (9-inch) Standard Pie Crusts
   (page 115), unbaked

Preheat oven to 400F (205C). In a large bowl, combine egg substitute, maple syrup granules, and butter until thoroughly blended. Stir in pecans. Pour into prepared pie crusts. Bake 50 to 60 minutes or until filling is set. Serve warm or at room temperature.

KRYSTINE'S
HEALTHY
GOURMET
BAKERY
COOKBOOK

100

OLD-FASHIONED PUMPKIN PIE

Makes 2 (9-inch) pies; 20 servings

This fabulous pie was a huge success over the holidays—Meg Ryan and Dennis Quaid purchased several. The filling is made without any fat or cholesterol! This is truly the best pumpkin pie I've ever tried, better than any with all the fat.

PER SERVING
Cal 204
Carb 35 gm
Prot 6 gm
Total fat 4 gm
Sat fat 2 gm
Cal from fat 18%
Chol 11 mg
Sodium 155 mg

1 (29-ounce) can pumpkin (3 2/3 cups)
1 cup egg substitute or egg whites
1 1/2 cups fructose or table sugar (sucrose)
1 teaspoon pure vanilla extract
3 1/2 teaspoons pumpkin pie spice

3 cups nonfat evaporated milk
2 (9-inch) Standard Pie Crusts
(page 115), Whole-Wheat Pastry
Crusts (page 111), or other crusts,
unbaked

Preheat oven to 400F (205C). In a large bowl, beat pumpkin, egg substitute, fructose, and vanilla with an electric mixer until combined. Stir in pumpkin pie spice and nonfat evaporated milk. Pour into prepared pie crusts. Bake 50 to 60 minutes or until a knife inserted off-center comes out clean. Serve warm or chilled.

BLACKBERRY-LEMON BRÛLÉE TART

Makes 1 tart; 12 servings

PER SERVING
Cal 435
Carb 75 gm
Prot 8 gm
Total fat 11 gm
Sat fat 3 gm
Cal from fat 23%
Chol 8 mg
Sodium 173 mg

A first-class dessert. A flaky pie crust is filled with lemon brûlée and blackberries, then topped with buttery oat-crunch topping.

LEMON BRÛLÉE
1/4 cup lemon extract
1/4 cup freshly squeezed lemon juice
1/2 cup unbleached all-purpose flour
1 cup nonfat (skim) milk
1/2 cup egg substitute

BLACKBERRY FILLING
4 cups fresh or frozen blackberries
1/2 cup unbleached all-purpose flour
1 1/2 cups fructose or table sugar (sucrose)
2 teaspoons pure vanilla extract

OATMEAL CRUNCH TOPPING
3 cups rolled oats
1/2 cup chopped pecans
1/3 cup unbleached all-purpose flour
6 tablespoons reduced-fat margarine
4 tablespoons maple syrup granules
    or brown sugar

ASSEMBLY
1 (10-inch) Standard Pie Crust
    (page 115), Flaky Tart Crust
    (page 112), or other crust, partially
    baked

Preheat oven to 375F (190C). Make brûlée: In a medium saucepan, whisk together all brûlée ingredients until all lumps dissolve. Cook over low heat, whisking constantly, until thickened, about 5 minutes.

Make filling: In a large bowl, gently toss together all filling ingredients. Make topping: In a medium bowl, with your fingers, mix all topping ingredients until thoroughly combined.

To assemble: Spoon brûlée into tart crust and spread evenly. Pour filling over brûlée and sprinkle with topping. Bake 25 to 35 minutes or until golden brown. Serve chilled.

KRYSTINE'S
HEALTHY
GOURMET
BAKERY
COOKBOOK

102

CHOCOLATE BROWNIE PUDDING TART

Makes 1 tart; 12 servings

A chocolate brownie crust filled with chocolate pudding—
intensely rich and satisfying!

PER SERVING
Cal 303
Carb 57 gm
Prot 9 gm
Total fat 4 gm
Sat fat 0 gm
Cal from fat 12%
Chol 1 mg
Sodium 100 mg

3/4 cup unbleached all-purpose flour
6 tablespoons unsweetened cocoa powder
1 1/2 cups fructose or table sugar (sucrose)
4 cups nonfat (skim) milk
1 1/2 cups liquid egg substitute

2 teaspoons pure vanilla extract
1/2 cup chocolate chips
1 (10-inch) Brownie Tart Crust
   (page 105), baked

Preheat oven to 375F (190C). Into a large saucepan, sift together flour, cocoa, and fructose. Stir in milk and egg substitute. Place pan in another pan containing boiling water or use a double boiler. Cook over low heat, stirring occasionally, 30 minutes. Remove from heat and stir in vanilla and chocolate chips. Pour into prepared crust.

Bake 10 minutes. Cool in refrigerator 2 hours before serving.

VARIATION
For a festive occasion, top with whipped cream and chocolate shavings.

CRANBERRY-APPLE MINI TARTS

Makes 4 mini tarts; 8 servings

A seasonal dessert at Krystine's Bakery, it is made October through January and is on our best-seller list. This is one you don't want to miss.

PER SERVING
Cal 223
Carb 32 gm
Prot 3 gm
Total fat 11 gm
Sat fat 2 gm
Cal from fat 49%
Chol 8 mg
Sodium 146 mg

4 cups peeled, sliced Granny Smith apples
3/4 cup whole fresh cranberries
1/2 cup apple juice concentrate
2 tablespoons ground cinnamon
Standard Pie Crusts (page 115) in
  4 mini tart pans, unbaked

TOPPING
1/2 cup unbleached all-purpose flour
1/4 cup maple syrup granules or
  granulated brown sugar
1/4 cup reduced-fat margarine
1/2 cup rolled oats
1/2 teaspoon ground cinnamon
1/2 cup finely chopped pecans

Preheat oven to 375F (190C). In a medium saucepan, cook apples, cranberries, apple juice concentrate, and cinnamon 10 minutes or until apples are soft, not mushy, stirring gently. Spoon filling into prepared tart crusts.

Make topping: In a small bowl, combine all topping ingredients. Mix with a pastry blender or your fingers until crumbly. Sprinkle topping over filling. Bake 15 to 20 minutes or until topping is golden brown. Serve warm or at room temperature.

KRYSTINE'S
HEALTHY
GOURMET
BAKERY
COOKBOOK

104

BROWNIE TART CRUST

Makes 1 (10-inch) tart crust

This delicious chocolatey crust will complement any custard or cream filling.

1/10 OF CRUST
Cal 128
Carb 14 gm
Prot 2 gm
Total fat 7 gm
Sat fat 4 gm
Cal from fat 52%
Chol 82 mg
Sodium 32 mg

1/3 cup butter
1/4 cup chocolate chips
2 tablespoons granulated or regular
brown sugar

2 tablespoons nonfat (skim) milk
1 cup unbleached all-purpose flour
1 teaspoon pure vanilla extract

Preheat oven to 375F (190C). Spray a 10-inch tart pan with vegetable oil spray. In a medium saucepan, combine butter, chocolate chips, brown sugar, and milk. Cook over low heat until chips are melted and mixture is smooth. Remove from heat, then whisk in flour and vanilla. Pour into prepared tart pan. Bake 30 minutes or until set.

MAPLE-PISTACHIO CRUST

Makes 1 (9-inch) crust

Wholesome, nutty, and lightly sweetened with a touch of maple syrup, this crust is perfect for that special-occasion pie.

1/10 OF CRUST
Cal 127
Carb 12 gm
Prot 5 gm
Total fat 7 gm
Sat fat 3 gm
Cal from fat 53%
Chol 9 mg
Sodium 37 mg

1/2 cup pistachios, chopped
2/3 cup wheat germ
2/3 cup whole-wheat flour
1/2 teaspoon ground cinnamon

1/4 teaspoon ground nutmeg
3 tablespoons butter
2 teaspoons maple syrup

Preheat oven to 375F (190C). Spray a 9-inch pie pan with vegetable oil spray. In a medium bowl, mix together all ingredients with a pastry blender or your fingers until crumbly. Press the crust onto the bottom and sides of prepared pan. Bake 25 to 30 minutes or until lightly browned.

KRYSTINE'S
HEALTHY
GOURMET
BAKERY
COOKBOOK

106

GRANOLA CRUNCH CRUST

Makes 1 (9-inch) crust

The wonderful crunch of granola and pecans will add a pleasing crispness to your crust—perfect with apple or peach filling.

2 cups granola
1/2 cup pecans

1/4 cup butter, melted
1/2 teaspoon ground cinnamon

Spray a 9-inch pie pan with vegetable oil spray. Blend granola and pecans in a blender or food processor until coarsely chopped. Add butter and cinnamon and blend until combined. Press the crust onto the bottom and sides of prepared pan. Chill before filling.

CREAM CHEESE CRUST

Makes 1 (9-inch) crust

This simple recipe is the perfect basic crust for fruit tarts or other summer fruit pies.

1/4 cup light cream cheese, softened
6 tablespoons butter, softened
1 cup unbleached all-purpose flour

1 tablespoon fructose or table sugar (sucrose)

In a medium bowl, combine cream cheese and butter using a pastry blender. Add flour and sugar and blend until thoroughly combined. Press onto bottom and sides of an ungreased 9-inch pie pan.

If baking without a filling, prick pastry all over with a fork and bake in a preheated 375F (190C) oven about 20 minutes or until lightly browned.

KRYSTINE'S
HEALTHY
GOURMET
BAKERY
COOKBOOK

108

GRAHAM CRACKER CRUST

Makes 1 (9-inch) crust

The most commonly used crust, it is always a favorite with cheesecakes.

1/10 OF CRUST
Cal 147
Carb 23 gm
Prot 2 gm
Total fat 5 gm
Sat fat 0.6 gm
Cal from fat 29%
Chol 0 mg
Sodium 73 mg

2 1/4 cups graham cracker crumbs
1/3 cup reduced-fat margarine, melted

1/4 cup maple syrup granules or
granulated brown sugar

In a medium bowl, mix together all ingredients until crumbly. Press onto bottom and sides of an ungreased 9-inch pie pan. Chill before filling.

CORNMEAL CRUST

Makes 1 (9- or 10-inch) crust

1/10 OF CRUST
Cal 190
Carb 17 gm
Prot 4 gm
Total fat 12 gm
Sat fat 6 gm
Cal from fat 56%
Chol 30 mg
Sodium 204 mg

For something a little different, try this with any fruit filling as a replacement for any traditional crust.

1 cup unbleached all-purpose flour
2/3 cup yellow or white cornmeal
1/8 teaspoon salt
8 tablespoons butter, chilled

2/3 cup light cream cheese, cut into
  small pieces
4 tablespoons ice water

In a medium bowl, whisk together flour, cornmeal, and salt. Cut in butter and cream cheese with a pastry blender until crumbly. Sprinkle in ice water, 1 tablespoon at a time, and gently toss with a fork until dough holds together.

Roll out dough on a lightly floured surface to a circle 3 inches larger than the pan. Fit circle into a pie pan. Flute edges with a fork or with your fingers.

If baking without a filling, prick pastry all over with a fork and bake in a preheated 375F (190C) oven about 20 minutes or until lightly browned.

KRYSTINE'S
HEALTHY
GOURMET
BAKERY
COOKBOOK

110

WHOLE-WHEAT PASTRY CRUST

Makes 2 (9-inch) crusts

A whole-grain healthy alternate to a regular basic crust, using only unbleached flour. A vegetarian favorite, it is great with tofu-based fillings.

1 cup whole-wheat pastry flour
1 cup unbleached all-purpose flour
1/2 teaspoon salt
1/4 teaspoon baking powder

7 tablespoons butter, chilled
6 tablespoons ice water
1 tablespoon freshly squeezed lemon
   juice

1/10 OF CRUST
Cal 79
Carb 9 gm
Prot 1 gm
Total fat 4 gm
Sat fat 2 gm
Cal from fat 45%
Chol 10 mg
Sodium 98 mg

Preheat oven to 375F (190C). Into a large bowl, sift together flours, salt, and baking powder. Add butter. Using a pastry blender or the tips of your fingers, rub in the butter until mixture resembles coarse cornmeal. Sprinkle with 3 tablespoons of the water and lemon juice and toss with a fork. Add more water, 1 tablespoon at a time, until dough holds together. Shape dough into 2 balls, cover with plastic wrap, and chill at least 30 minutes before rolling.

Roll out each ball between sheets of waxed paper to 1/4-inch thickness. Fit dough into pie pans.

If baking without a filling, prick pastry all over with a fork. Bake in a preheated 375F (190C) oven about 20 minutes or until lightly browned.

FLAKY TART CRUST

Makes 1 (10-inch) tart crust

A very popular, versatile crust that can be filled with any fruit or custard filling. The only thing that might not fit into this crust is your imagination.

1/3 cup nonfat cream cheese, softened
1/2 cup butter, softened

1 cup unbleached all-purpose flour

Preheat oven to 375F (190C). In a medium bowl, using a pastry blender, combine cream cheese and butter. Add flour, then incorporate until thoroughly combined. Press into ungreased 10-inch tart pan. Bake 20 minutes or until lightly browned.

KRYSTINE'S
HEALTHY
GOURMET
BAKERY
COOKBOOK

112

MACADAMIA NUT CRUST

Makes 1 (9-inch) crust

A crunchy crust filled with macadamia nuts in every bite—a must for exotic cheesecakes.

1/4 cup unbleached all-purpose flour
1/2 cup fructose or table sugar (sucrose)
1/4 cup reduced-fat margarine, melted

1 cup macadamia nuts, roasted
(see Note, page 31), chopped

1/10 OF CRUST
Cal 173
Carb 16 gm
Prot 2 gm
Total fat 12 gm
Sat fat 2 gm
Cal from fat 63%
Chol 0 mg
Sodium 56 mg

In a large bowl combine all ingredients and mix thoroughly using your fingers. Pat firmly into a 9-inch springform pan. Freeze at least 15 minutes before filling.

NONFAT MERINGUE CRUST

Fill this very simple-to-make no-fat crust with nonfat banana custard (page 98) and your entire dessert will be fat free.

1/10 OF CRUST
Cal 80
Carb 18 gm
Prot 1 gm
Total fat 0 gm
Sat fat 0 gm
Cal from fat 0%
Chol 0 mg
Sodium 22 mg

4 egg whites
3/4 cup fructose or table sugar (sucrose)

1/4 teaspoon cream of tartar
1 teaspoon pure vanilla extract

Preheat oven to 300F (150C). Spray a 9-inch pie pan with vegetable oil spray. In a small bowl, beat egg whites until frothy. Add cream of tartar. Beat until stiff. Gradually add fructose and beat until glossy. Stir in vanilla. Turn into prepared pan. Bake 1 hour or until firm.

KRYSTINE'S
HEALTHY
GOURMET
BAKERY
COOKBOOK

114

STANDARD PIE CRUSTS

Makes 2 (9-inch) deep pie crusts, 6 mini tarts, or 1 (12-inch) tart crust

A very flaky, versatile crust that goes with just about any pie filling.

2 cups unbleached all-purpose flour
1/2 teaspoon salt

6 tablespoons butter, softened
6 tablespoons ice water

Preheat oven to 400F (205C). Combine flour, salt, and butter with pastry blender until crumbly. Add water and mix with a fork until dough holds together.

For 2 (9-inch) crusts, divide dough into 2 balls. Place 1 ball on a board sprinkled with flour. Roll out dough into an 11-inch circle. Fit circle into a pie pan. Crimp the edges by pressing down with a fork.

If baking without a filling, prick pastry all over with a fork. Bake 15 minutes or until light brown.

VARIATION
For 1 (9-inch) pie crust or 1 (10-inch) tart crust; cut recipe ingredients in half.

1/10 OF CRUST
Cal 38
Carb 5 gm
Prot 0.6 gm
Total fat 2 gm
Sat fat 1 gm
Cal from fat 47%
Chol 5 mg
Sodium 44 mg

WHOLESOME
WHOLE-WHEAT CRUST

Makes 1 (9-inch) crust

This crust is fabulous with fresh fruit fillings, such as peach or apple.
It tastes very healthy and delicious.

1 cup wheat germ
2/3 cup whole-wheat flour
1/2 teaspoon ground cinnamon

1/4 teaspoon ground nutmeg
4 tablespoons fruit juice concentrate
or honey

Preheat oven to 400F (205C). Spray a 9-inch pie pan with vegetable oil spray. In a medium bowl, mix together wheat germ, flour, cinnamon, and nutmeg. Add fruit concentrate and work ingredients with your fingers until crumbly. Press onto bottom and sides of prepared pan. Bake 10 minutes or until browned.

KRYSTINE'S
HEALTHY
GOURMET
BAKERY
COOKBOOK

116

CAKES

This chapter contains my essential cake collection. It is a repertoire of bakery best-sellers and old family recipes. You'll find coffeecakes, traditional layer cakes, cupcakes, upside-down cakes, and mini-Bundt cakes, all of which are reduced in cholesterol. (There are no egg yolks in any recipe.)

Many have no added fat; some are considerably reduced in fat; and a few have been created in a traditional manner, with good old-fashioned butter. The majority of the recipes call for unbleached all-purpose flour rather than bleached cake flour. You will find a few of the recipes do call for bleached cake flour. This is partly due to the fact that traditional layer cakes do demand the light and delicate texture that only bleached cake flour can impart. It is possible to create your own cake flour from unbleached flour by exchanging 2 tablespoons for 2 tablespoons of cornstarch per cup of all-purpose flour.

I believe after trying these recipes you'll come to the realization that you will never make a boxed cake again.

ORANGE-SCENTED
ANGEL FOOD CAKE

Makes 14 servings

PER SERVING
Cal 148
Carb 32 gm
Prot 4 gm
Total fat 0 gm
Sat fat 0 gm
Cal from fat 0%
Chol 0 mg
Sodium 86 mg

A light, airy cake with just a whisper of freshly squeezed orange rind. I love the fact that angel food cake is always made with egg whites and has no added fat. This recipe includes orange juice concentrate, which adds a sharp blast of orange flavor to every bite.

12 egg whites, at room temperature

1 1/2 teaspoons cream of tartar

1/4 teaspoon salt

1 1/4 cups fructose or table sugar (sucrose)

1 1/4 cups cake flour

1/2 cup frozen orange juice concentrate, thawed

2 tablespoons freshly grated orange rind

Preheat oven to 350F (175C). In a large bowl, beat egg whites and cream of tartar with an electric mixer until soft peaks form when the beaters are raised. Gradually beat in salt and fructose. Beat until very stiff peaks form when the beaters are raised. Gently stir in flour, orange concentrate, and orange rind.

Pour batter into an ungreased 10-inch tube pan. Bake 40 minutes or until a wooden pick inserted into center comes out clean. To cool cake, invert pan and cool completely, using a funnel to keep cake from touching the countertop, if necessary. Use a spatula to separate cooled cake from pan.

KRYSTINE'S
HEALTHY
GOURMET
BAKERY
COOKBOOK
118

NONFAT PLAIN YELLOW CAKE

Makes 14 servings

I came up with this recipe for my mother, who has been after me over the last few years to come up with "just a plain yellow cake that isn't fattening." Mom, this one's for you! This cake also goes well with almost any chocolate frosting.
The method for making the cake is slightly different, but the results are great.

PER SERVING
Cal 134
Carb 29 gm
Prot 3 gm
Total fat 0.4 gm
Sat fat 0 gm
Cal from fat 3%
Chol 0 mg
Sodium 55 mg

1 1/4 cups cake flour
1 teaspoon baking powder
1/4 teaspoon salt
4 egg whites
1/4 cup vegetable oil
1 1/4 cups fructose or table sugar
  (sucrose)

1/2 cup liquid egg substitute or
  egg whites
1 cup boiling water
2 drops yellow food coloring (optional)

Preheat oven to 350F (175C). Spray a 10-inch tube pan generously with vegetable oil spray. Into a small bowl, sift together flour, baking powder, and salt; set aside.

In a large bowl, beat egg whites with an electric mixer until stiff. Add oil, fructose, and liquid egg substitute and beat 1 minute. Add hot water and food coloring, if using, and mix until incorporated. Add flour mixture to egg mixture and beat until smooth.

Pour batter into prepared pan. Bake 35 to 40 minutes or until a wooden pick inserted into center comes out clean. Cool cake in pan 10 minutes, then turn out onto a wire rack to finish cooling.

LOW-FAT LEMON
YOGURT CAKE

Makes 14 servings

This light, refreshing lemon cake is extremely popular during the summer months. It is made with low-fat yogurt to reduce fat intake so you can have seconds without feeling guilty.

1 1/4 cups cake flour
1/2 teaspoon baking powder
1/2 teaspoon baking soda
1/4 teaspoon salt
1/3 cup reduced-fat margarine
1/4 cup low-fat lemon yogurt
3/4 cup fructose or table sugar (sucrose)

1 cup egg whites or liquid egg substitute
3 tablespoons freshly squeezed lemon juice
1 teaspoon lemon extract
1 tablespoon freshly grated lemon rind
Lemon Love Note Glaze (page 185)

Preheat oven to 350F (175C). Spray a 10-inch tube pan generously with vegetable oil spray. Into a small bowl, sift together flour, baking powder, baking soda, and salt; set aside.

In a large bowl, beat margarine, yogurt, fructose, egg whites, lemon juice, lemon extract, and lemon rind with an electric mixer until smooth and creamy. Add flour mixture to yogurt mixture and mix until thoroughly combined.

Pour batter into prepared pan. Bake 35 minutes or until a wooden pick inserted into center comes out clean. Cool cake in pan 10 minutes, then turn out onto a wire rack. Pour glaze over warm cake and finish cooling.

KRYSTINE'S
HEALTHY
GOURMET
BAKERY
COOKBOOK

120

POPPY SEED-LEMON CAKE

Makes 14 servings

Anything with poppy seeds always seems to be popular with my customers and this Bundt cake is no exception. A velvety lemon cake surrounded by a tangy, sweet, lemony syrup makes this dessert undeniably decadent.

PER SERVING
Cal 332
Carb 61 gm
Prot 5 gm
Total fat 8 gm
Sat fat 4 gm
Cal from fat 22%
Chol 18 mg
Sodium 186 mg

3 cups cake flour
1/2 teaspoon baking soda
1/2 teaspoon baking powder
1/4 teaspoon salt
1/2 cup butter, softened
2 cups fructose or table sugar (sucrose)
1/2 cup nonfat lemon yogurt
3/4 cup egg whites or liquid egg substitute
1 cup nonfat (skim) milk
2 tablespoons freshly squeezed lemon juice
2 tablespoons freshly grated lemon rind
1 tablespoon white vinegar
3 tablespoons poppy seeds

LEMON SYRUP
1/3 cup fructose or table sugar (sucrose)
1/3 cup freshly squeezed lemon juice

Preheat oven to 350F (175C). Spray a 10-inch tube pan generously with vegetable oil spray. Into a small bowl, sift together flour, baking soda, baking powder, and salt; set aside.

In a large bowl, beat butter and fructose with an electric mixer until light. Add yogurt, egg whites, milk, lemon juice, lemon rind, vinegar, and poppy seeds and beat until incorporated. Add flour mixture to butter mixture and beat until thoroughly combined, about 1 minute.

Pour batter into prepared pan. Bake 1 hour and 15 minutes or until a wooden pick inserted into center comes out clean.

While cake is baking, make syrup: In a small bowl, combine fructose and lemon juice. Cool cake in pan 10 minutes, then turn out onto a wire rack. Pour glaze over warm cake and finish cooling.

CHOCOLATE TOFU CUPCAKES

Makes 18 cupcakes

PER CUPCAKE
Cal 180
Carb 26 gm
Prot 4 gm
Total fat 7 gm
Sat fat 3 gm
Cal from fat 35%
Chol 14 mg
Sodium 144 mg

Making these cupcakes is always an exciting experience. My kids love them yet have no idea about the hidden tofu these delightful chocolate pleasures contain. I feel really good about giving these to them. If desired, Milk Chocolate Frosting (page 177) goes great on these.

2 cups unbleached all-purpose flour

1/3 cup unsweetened cocoa powder

2 teaspoons baking powder

1/2 cup butter, softened

1 cup packed light brown sugar

1/2 cup mashed tofu

1 cup nonfat cottage cheese, drained

1 teaspoon pure vanilla extract

1/2 cup chocolate chips

Preheat oven to 350F (175C). Place paper cupcake liners in 18 muffin cups. Into a small bowl, sift together flour, cocoa, and baking powder; set aside.

In a large bowl, beat butter, sugar, tofu, cottage cheese, and vanilla until smooth. Add flour mixture to tofu mixture and beat until thoroughly combined. Stir in chocolate chips.

Fill paper-lined cups half full. Bake 15 minutes or until a wooden pick inserted into centers comes out clean. Cool on a wire rack.

KRYSTINE'S
HEALTHY
GOURMET
BAKERY
COOKBOOK

122

CHOCOLATE CHIP-LEMON CAKE

Makes 14 servings

My dear friend Suzie Caron adores the combination of lemon and dark chocolate. She is the inspiration for this luscious, supermoist dessert. Chocolate chips enhance the lemon flavor beautifully. This cake will warm your heart as Suzie does mine.

PER SERVING
Cal 324
Carb 55 gm
Prot 5 gm
Total fat 10 gm
Sat fat 6 gm
Cal from fat 28%
Chol 18 mg
Sodium 267 mg

2 cups cake flour
1 teaspoon baking powder
1 teaspoon baking soda
1/2 teaspoon salt
1/2 cup butter, softened
3/4 cup fructose or table sugar (sucrose)
1 cup egg whites or liquid egg substitute

1 cup low-fat lemon yogurt
1 teaspoon pure vanilla extract
2 tablespoons freshly squeezed lemon
  juice
1 tablespoon freshly grated lemon rind
1 cup chocolate chips
Citrus Glaze (page 186)

Preheat oven to 350F (175C). Spray a 10-inch tube pan with vegetable oil spray and dust with flour. Into a small bowl, sift together flour, baking powder, baking soda, and salt; set aside.

In a large bowl, beat butter and fructose with an electric mixer until light and creamy. Add egg whites, yogurt, vanilla, lemon juice, and lemon rind and beat until incorporated. Add flour mixture to yogurt mixture and beat until smooth. Stir in chocolate chips.

Pour batter into prepared pan. Bake 35 to 40 minutes or until a wooden pick inserted into center comes out clean. Cool cake in pan 10 minutes, then turn out onto a wire rack. Pour glaze over warm cake and finish cooling.

MAUI PINEAPPLE CAKE

Makes 12 servings

PER SERVING
WITH FROSTING
Cal 340
Carb 59 gm
Prot 5 gm
Total fat 10 gm
Sat fat 5 gm
Cal from fat 26%
Chol 24 mg
Sodium 298 mg

This cake was inspired by my love for sweet Maui pineapple. If fresh fruit is unavailable, you may substitute crushed canned pineapple.

2 cups cake flour
2 teaspoons baking soda
1/2 cup butter, softened
1 cup fructose or table sugar (sucrose)
1 cup maple syrup granules or
   granulated brown sugar

1/2 cup egg whites or liquid egg substitute
2 1/2 cups fresh pineapple, crushed or
   finely chopped and drained
1 cup chopped macadamia nuts (optional)
Pineapple Cream Cheese Frosting
   (page 168)

Preheat oven to 350F (175C). Spray 2 (9-inch-round) cake pans with vegetable oil spray and dust with flour. Into a small bowl, sift together flour and baking soda; set aside.

In a large bowl, beat butter, fructose, and maple syrup granules with an electric mixer until light and creamy. Add egg whites and pineapple and mix well. Add flour mixture to butter mixture and beat until incorporated. Stir in macadamia nuts, if using.

Pour batter into prepared pans. Bake 20 to 25 minutes or until a wooden pick inserted into cake centers comes out clean. Cool cakes in pans 10 minutes, then turn out onto a wire rack to finish cooling. Frost and fill cake with frosting. Refrigerate leftovers.

KRYSTINE'S
HEALTHY
GOURMET
BAKERY
COOKBOOK

124

LOW-FAT, FLOURLESS,
CHOCOLATE TRUFFLE CAKE

Makes 10 to 12 servings

Our number-one seller during Passover, this cake literally melts in your mouth. It has intense, full chocolate flavor without all the fat of the traditional chocolate cake. Serve with a dollop of whipped topping and fresh ripe raspberries.

3/4 cup chocolate chips, finely chopped
1 large egg white
1/8 teaspoon cream of tartar
3/4 cup unsweetened cocoa powder

2/3 cup fructose or table sugar (sucrose)
3/4 cup low-fat evaporated milk
1 cup egg whites or liquid egg substitute
1 teaspoon pure vanilla extract

Preheat oven to 350F (175C). Spray a 9-inch springform pan with vegetable oil spray. Place chopped chocolate chips in a large bowl; set aside. In a small bowl, beat 1 egg white with cream of tartar until stiff peaks form; set aside.

In a medium saucepan, heat cocoa, fructose, and milk until simmering, stirring constantly. Remove from heat and pour over chocolate chips. Whisk in 1 cup egg whites, then fold in beaten egg white.

Pour batter into prepared pan and set in another pan at least 2 inches wider and deeper. Add enough water to bottom pan to come two-thirds up the side of the cake pan. (This is so edges won't burn.) Bake 30 minutes. Chill in refrigerator 8 hours before serving.

OLD-FASHIONED
GERMAN CHOCOLATE CAKE

Makes 12 servings

PER SERVING
WITH FROSTING
Cal 608
Carb 93 gm
Prot 10 gm
Total fat 23 gm
Sat fat 9 gm
Cal from fat 34%
Chol 33 mg
Sodium 357 mg

Of all the cakes in the world, German Chocolate is my all-time favorite. Because of its high fat content, I indulge only once a year, every birthday. With a scoop of vanilla ice cream and fresh whipped cream, I am a happy girl! This recipe has been in my family for decades. It is as good as they get.

3 cups cake flour
2 teaspoons baking powder
1/4 teaspoon salt
2/3 cup butter, softened
1 cup fructose or table sugar (sucrose)
1 cup maple syrup granules or
    granulated brown sugar
1/2 cup egg whites or liquid egg substitute

1 cup nonfat (skim) milk
1/3 cup coffee
2 squares (2 ounces) unsweetened
    chocolate
1 teaspoon pure vanilla extract
Maple Coconut-Pecan Frosting
    (page 166)

Preheat oven to 350F (175C). Spray 2 (9-inch-round) cake pans with vegetable oil spray and dust with flour. Into a small bowl, sift together flour, baking powder, and salt; set aside.

In a large bowl, beat butter, fructose, and maple syrup granules with an electric mixer until light and fluffy. Add egg whites and beat 30 seconds. Add flour mixture and milk alternately to the butter mixture, beating after each addition. Add coffee and vanilla and mix well.

Pour batter into prepared pans. Bake 30 minutes or until a wooden pick inserted into cake centers comes out clean. Cool cakes in pans 10 minutes, then turn out onto a wire rack to finish cooling. Frost and fill cake with frosting. Refrigerate leftovers.

KRYSTINE'S
HEALTHY
GOURMET
BAKERY
COOKBOOK

126

COCONUT CUSTARD CAKE

Makes 12 servings

Made with coconut milk, this coconut cake has a creamy coconut filling. It is one of the best desserts I've created. Swathed in Vanilla Buttercream Frosting, this cake is simply outstanding.

PER SERVING
WITHOUT
FROSTING
Cal 401
Carb 66 gm
Prot 6 gm
Total fat 11 gm
Sat fat 9 gm
Cal from fat 25%
Chol 12 mg
Sodium 328 mg

3 cups cake flour
2 1/2 teaspoons baking powder
1 teaspoon baking soda
1/2 teaspoon salt
1/2 cup butter, softened
1 1/2 cups fructose or table sugar (sucrose)
1/4 cup nonfat plain yogurt
1/2 cup egg whites or liquid egg substitute

1 cup reduced-fat or regular coconut milk
  (fresh or canned)
2 teaspoons pure vanilla extract
1 1/2 cups sweetened flaked coconut
1/2 recipe Coconut Cream Filling
  (page 189)
Vanilla Buttercream Frosting (page 175)
  (optional)

Preheat oven to 350F (175C). Generously spray 2 (9-inch-round) cake pans with vegetable oil spray and dust with flour. Into a small bowl, sift together flour, baking powder, baking soda, and salt; set aside.

In a large bowl, beat butter and fructose with an electric mixer until light. Add yogurt, egg whites, coconut milk, vanilla, and flaked coconut and beat until smooth. Add flour mixture to coconut mixture and beat about 1 minute.

Pour batter into prepared pans. Bake 20 minutes or until a wooden pick inserted into cake centers comes out clean. Cool cakes in pans 10 minutes, then turn out onto a wire rack to finish cooling. Fill cake with Coconut Cream Filling. Frost with Vanilla Buttercream Frosting, if desired. Refrigerate leftovers.

OLD-FASHIONED SPICE CAKE

Makes 12 servings

Supermoist with a hint of spice, this cake is a wonderful choice for family gatherings or important occasions.

2 cups cake flour
1 teaspoon baking soda
1/2 teaspoon salt
2 teaspoons ground cinnamon
1/2 teaspoon ground cloves
1 teaspoon ground allspice
1/2 teaspoon ground nutmeg

1/4 teaspoon ground ginger
1/2 cup butter, softened
2 cups maple syrup granules or
　granulated brown sugar
1 cup low-fat buttermilk
1/2 cup egg whites or liquid egg substitute
Maple Buttercream Frosting (page 173)

Preheat oven to 350F (175C). Generously spray 2 (9-inch-round) pans with vegetable oil spray. Into a small bowl, sift together flour, baking soda, salt, cinnamon, cloves, allspice, nutmeg, and ginger; set aside.

In a large bowl, beat butter and maple syrup granules with an electric mixer until light and creamy. Add buttermilk, egg whites, and flour mixture and beat until combined.

Pour batter into prepared pans. Bake 25 minutes or until a wooden pick inserted into cake centers comes out clean. Cool cakes in pans 10 minutes, then turn out onto a wire rack to finish cooling. Frost with Maple Buttercream Frosting.

KRYSTINE'S
HEALTHY
GOURMET
BAKERY
COOKBOOK

128

NONFAT APPLE-CARROT CAKE

Makes 14 servings

You'll find no butter or oil in this dense, moist cake filled with fresh apples and carrots. Nonfat mayonnaise is the winning substitute.

PER SERVING
WITHOUT
FROSTING
Cal 265
Carb 52 gm
Prot 4 gm
Total fat 0.5 gm
Sat fat 0 gm
Cal from fat 1%
Chol 0 mg
Sodium 246 mg

3 cups unbleached all-purpose flour
2 teaspoons baking soda
1 1/2 teaspoons ground cinnamon
1/2 teaspoon ground nutmeg
1/4 teaspoon salt
1 1/2 cups fructose or table sugar (sucrose)
3/4 cup nonfat mayonnaise

1/4 cup unsweetened applesauce
1/3 cup nonfat (skim) milk
1/2 cup egg whites or liquid egg substitute
3 cups peeled, diced Granny Smith apples
1 cup grated carrots
Low-Fat Cream Cheese Frosting
   (page 170) (optional)

Preheat oven to 350F (175C). Generously spray a 10-inch tube pan with vegetable oil spray. Into a small bowl, sift together flour, baking soda, cinnamon, nutmeg and salt; set aside.

In a large bowl, beat fructose, mayonnaise, applesauce, milk, and egg whites with an electric mixer until thoroughly blended. Add flour mixture to mayonnaise mixture and stir until combined. Fold in apples and carrots.

Pour batter into prepared pan. Bake 55 minutes or until a wooden pick inserted into center comes out clean. Cool cake in pan 10 minutes, then turn out onto a wire rack to finish cooling. Frost with Low-Fat Cream Cheese Frosting, if desired.

PAULA JEAN'S RED CAKE

Makes 10 servings

PER SERVING
WITH FROSTING
Cal 468
Carb 69 gm
Prot 6 gm
Total fat 19 gm
Sat fat 11 gm
Cal from fat 36%
Chol 50 mg
Sodium 384 mg

This supermoist cake made with a touch of cocoa has been a family favorite for generations, especially among the children. Although I've reduced the fat from the original recipe, rest assured that it's equally as yummy.

2 cups cake flour	1/4 cup maple syrup granules or
1 teaspoon baking soda	granulated brown sugar
1 teaspoon baking powder	1/2 cup egg whites or liquid egg substitute
2 tablespoons unsweetened cocoa powder	1/4 cup nonfat plain yogurt
1/2 teaspoon salt	1 cup nonfat (skim) milk
1/8 teaspoon red food coloring	1 1/2 tablespoons apple cider vinegar
1/2 cup butter, softened	1 teaspoon pure vanilla extract
1 cup fructose or table sugar (sucrose)	Fluffy White Frosting (page 181)

Preheat oven to 350F (175C). Generously spray 2 (8-inch-round) cake pans with vegetable oil spray and dust with flour. Into a small bowl, sift together flour, baking soda, baking powder, cocoa, and salt. Whisk in red food coloring; set aside.

In a large bowl, beat butter, fructose, and maple syrup granules with an electric mixer until light. Add egg whites, yogurt, milk, vinegar, and vanilla. Beat until smooth. Add flour mixture to butter mixture and beat until well blended.

Pour batter into prepared pans. Bake 20 to 25 minutes or until a wooden pick inserted into cake centers comes out clean. Cool cakes in pans 10 minutes, then turn out onto a wire rack to finish cooling. Frost and fill with frosting.

VARIATION
Pour batter into 24 greased muffin cups and bake 12 to 15 minutes.

KRYSTINE'S
HEALTHY
GOURMET
BAKERY
COOKBOOK

130

HOT APPLESAUCE-
DATE CAKE

Makes 10 servings

A spicy, deep, dark, moist cake loaded with dates and hot applesauce that will titillate your taste buds. Whole-wheat flour adds a wholesome touch.

PER SERVING
Cal 329
Carb 46 gm
Prot 6 gm
Total fat 16 gm
Sat fat 6 gm
Cal from fat 44%
Chol 25 mg
Sodium 282 mg

2 cups whole-wheat pastry flour
2 teaspoons baking soda
1 teaspoon ground cinnamon
1/2 teaspoon ground nutmeg
1/2 teaspoon ground allspice
1/2 cup liquid egg substitute or egg whites
1 cup maple syrup granules or
    granulated brown sugar, plus
    2 tablespoons for sprinkling

1/2 cup unsalted butter, softened
2 cups unsweetened applesauce,
    heated until hot
1 cup chopped dates
3/4 cup chopped walnuts

Preheat oven to 350F (165C). Spray a 9-inch-round cake pan with vegetable oil spray. In a small bowl, stir together flour, baking soda, cinnamon, nutmeg, and allspice; set aside.

In a large bowl, beat egg substitute, 1 cup maple syrup granules, and butter with an electric mixer until combined. Add applesauce, dates, and walnuts and beat 1 minute. Add applesauce mixture to flour mixture and beat 1 minute.

Pour batter into prepared pan. Bake 50 minutes or until a wooden pick inserted into center comes out clean. While cake is still warm, sprinkle with remaining 2 tablespoons maple syrup granules. Cool in pan on a wire rack.

NONFAT CARROT CAKE

Makes 10 servings

PER SERVING
Cal 315
Carb 71 gm
Prot 7 gm
Total fat 0.5 gm
Sat fat 0 gm
Cal from fat 1%
Chol 0 mg
Sodium 223 mg

For having no added fat, this carrot cake is superb. Be careful not to overbeat, for this is a very delicate cake. Serve with nonfat vanilla frozen yogurt or frost with Nonfat Vanilla Yogurt Filling (page 188).

2 cups unbleached all-purpose flour
1 3/4 cups fructose or table sugar (sucrose)
2 teaspoons baking soda
1 teaspoon ground cinnamon
1 cup nonfat plain yogurt
3/4 cup liquid egg substitute or egg whites

2/3 cup pureed cooked carrots or baby-food carrots
2/3 cup chopped pineapple
1/2 cup golden raisins
Maple syrup granules

Preheat oven to 350F (175C). Spray 2 (8-inch-round) cake pans with vegetable oil spray. Into a small bowl, sift together flour, fructose, baking soda, and cinnamon; set aside.

In a large bowl, beat yogurt and egg substitute until smooth. Add flour mixture and stir until combined. Fold in carrot puree, pineapple, and raisins.

Pour batter into prepared pans. Bake 30 to 40 minutes or until a wooden pick inserted into cake centers comes out clean. Cool cake in pan 10 minutes, then turn out onto a wire rack. Sprinkle tops with maple syrup granules while cakes are warm.

KRYSTINE'S
HEALTHY
GOURMET
BAKERY
COOKBOOK

132

NONFAT CHOCOLATE
DEVASTATION CAKE

Makes 10 servings

This is the cake I prepared on "The Suzanne Somers Show." Emma Samms and Suzanne gobbled it up right on camera. When you try this magnificent cake, you're not going to believe it has no added fat. I must thank Auntie Paula for contributing this winning recipe.

PER SERVING
WITH FROSTING
Cal 315
Carb 72 gm
Prot 4 gm
Total fat 0.4 gm
Sat fat 0 gm
Cal from fat 1%
Chol 0 mg
Sodium 195 mg

2 cups cake flour
1 cup maple syrup granules, fructose, or
    table sugar (sucrose)
1/3 cup unsweetened cocoa powder
2 teaspoons baking soda
1 cup nonfat plain yogurt

1/4 cup egg whites or liquid egg substitute
1 cup water
1 tablespoon apple cider vinegar
1 tablespoon pure vanilla extract
Nonfat Chocolate Frosting (page 183)

Preheat oven to 350F (175C). Generously spray a 9-inch-round cake pan with vegetable oil spray. Into a medium bowl, sift together flour, maple syrup granules, cocoa, and baking soda; set aside.

In a large bowl, beat yogurt, egg whites, water, vinegar, and vanilla until blended. Add flour mixture to yogurt mixture and beat with an electric mixer until thoroughly combined, about 3 minutes.

Pour batter into prepared pan. Bake 35 to 45 minutes or until a wooden pick inserted into center comes out clean. Let cool in pan 10 minutes, then remove cake from pan to a plate. Pour warm frosting over warm cake and let set before serving.

FRESH ORANGE JUICE CUPCAKES

Makes 24 cupcakes

PER CUPCAKE
WITH FROSTING
Cal 201
Carb 35 gm
Prot 5 gm
Total fat 5 gm
Sat fat 2 gm
Cal from fat 22%
Chol 8 mg
Sodium 115 mg

These special treats burst with tangy orange flavor. Freshly squeezed orange juice is what makes them so delicious.

2 1/2 cups unbleached all-purpose flour
2 teaspoons baking powder
1/4 cup nonfat plain yogurt
1/4 cup vegetable oil
2 teaspoons orange extract
3 teaspoons freshly grated orange rind
1 1/2 cups fructose or table sugar
  (sucrose)

3/4 cup liquid egg substitute
3/4 cup freshly squeezed orange juice
1/2 cup nonfat (skim) milk
Orange Buttercream Frosting
  (page 182)

Preheat oven to 325F (165C). Line 24 muffin cups with paper cupcake liners. Into a small bowl, sift together flour and baking powder; set aside.

In a large bowl beat yogurt, oil, orange extract, orange rind, and fructose with an electric mixer until thoroughly combined. Add egg substitute and mix well. Add yogurt mixture alternately with orange juice and milk to flour mixture. Beat about 3 minutes or until smooth.

Fill paper-lined cups two-thirds full. Bake 12 minutes or until a wooden pick inserted in centers comes out clean. Cool 30 to 45 minutes. Top with frosting.

KRYSTINE'S
HEALTHY
GOURMET
BAKERY
COOKBOOK
134

NONFAT PINEAPPLE
UPSIDE-DOWN CAKE

Makes 10 servings

This cake is just like the classic version minus all the fat. At the bakery, we have a few variations of this recipe. By substituting apples and cranberries or perhaps peaches and blueberries for the pineapple, you can create many different upside-down cakes by simply changing the fruit. After you taste one, you still won't believe something so delectable and moist is truly **FAT FREE.**

PER SERVING
Cal 297
Carb 66 gm
Prot 6 gm
Total fat 0.5 gm
Sat fat 0 gm
Cal from fat 1%
Chol 0 mg
Sodium 170 mg

2 cups unbleached all-purpose flour
1 teaspoon baking soda
1 teaspoon baking powder
1/2 cup unsweetened applesauce
1 1/2 cups fructose or sugar
1 teaspoon pure vanilla extract

1 cup liquid egg substitute
3/4 cup nonfat (skim) milk mixed with
 1 tablespoon apple cider vinegar
2 cups diced fresh pineapple, drained
1/3 cup maple syrup granules or
 granulated brown sugar

Preheat oven to 350F (175C). Spray a 9-inch-round cake pan with vegetable oil spray. Into a small bowl, sift together flour, baking soda, and baking powder; set aside.

In a large bowl, beat together applesauce, fructose, and vanilla with an electric mixer until smooth. Add egg substitute, 1/4 cup at a time, beating well after each addition. Add flour mixture alternately with sour milk and applesauce mixture, beating after each addition.

Spread drained pineapple in prepared cake pan. Pour batter over pineapple. Bake 50 to 60 minutes or until a wooden pick inserted in center comes out clean. Cool 30 to 40 minutes or until pan is no longer hot to the touch. Invert pan and turn out onto a plate. Sprinkle with maple syrup granules while still warm.

BANANA, CHOCOLATE CHIP, TOFU MINI BUNDT CAKES

Makes 10 mini Bundt cakes

PER CAKE
Cal 518
Carb 87 gm
Prot 9 gm
Total fat 16 gm
Sat fat 2 gm
Cal from fat 28%
Chol 0 mg
Sodium 119 mg

We make these dairy-free, egg-free, Bundt cakes—our number-one wholesale item—by the hundreds every week. Full of banana flavor, tofu, chocolate chips, and no cholesterol, so you know you're eating something good.

4 cups unbleached all-purpose flour
1 teaspoon baking soda
1 teaspoon baking powder
1/2 cup vegetable oil
1 1/4 cups fructose or table sugar (sucrose)

2 cups mashed ripe bananas
1 1/4 cups mashed tofu
2/3 cup chocolate chips
1 teaspoon pure vanilla extract

Preheat oven to 350F (175C). Generously spray 10 mini Bundt pans with vegetable oil spray. In a large bowl, whisk together flour, baking soda, and baking powder. Add oil, fructose, bananas, tofu, chocolate chips, and vanilla and stir until thoroughly combined. Do not overbeat.

Pour batter into prepared pans, filling each half full. Bake 30 minutes or until a wooden pick inserted into cake centers comes out clean. Cool cakes in pans 10 minutes, then turn out onto a wire rack to finish cooling.

KRYSTINE'S
HEALTHY
GOURMET
BAKERY
COOKBOOK

136

PUMPKIN-APPLE
MINI BUNDT CAKES

Makes 6 mini Bundt cakes

Pumpkin and apples are combined to make moist, dense little Bundt cakes, fragrant with spices and most pleasing to the palate. If mini Bundt pans are not available, you may use large muffin cups.

PER CAKE
Cal 350
Carb 62 gm
Prot 7 gm
Total fat 10 gm
Sat fat 1 gm
Cal from fat 26%
Chol 0 mg
Sodium 188 mg

1 cup unbleached all-purpose flour
1 teaspoon baking soda
1 tablespoon ground cinnamon
1 teaspoon ground nutmeg
1/4 teaspoon ground mace
1/4 cup vegetable oil
1 cup maple syrup granules or
   granulated brown sugar

2/3 cup egg whites or liquid egg
   substitute
1 cup canned pumpkin
2 cups peeled, diced, Granny Smith
   apples
3/4 cup golden raisins
1/2 cup chopped walnuts (optional)

Preheat oven to 350F (175C). Generously spray 6 mini Bundt pans with vegetable oil spray. Into a small bowl, sift together flour, baking soda, cinnamon, nutmeg, and mace; set aside.

In a medium bowl, beat oil, maple syrup granules, egg whites, and pumpkin until thoroughly combined. Add flour mixture to pumpkin mixture and mix until combined. Stir in apples, raisins, and walnuts, if using.

Pour batter into prepared pans. Bake 25 to 30 minutes or until a wooden pick inserted into cake centers comes out clean. Cool in pans 30 minutes, then turn out onto a wire rack to finish cooling.

NONFAT BLUEBERRY-BANANA MINI BUNDT CAKES

Makes 12 mini Bundt cakes

PER CAKE
Cal 250
Carb 56 gm
Prot 5 gm
Total fat 0.4 gm
Sat fat 0 gm
Cal from fat 3%
Chol 0 mg
Sodium 141 mg

Unlike most fat-free cakes, which are rubbery, this wonderfully light, supermoist Bundt cake has an exquisite texture. It can be served for breakfast or as an after-dinner dessert.

2 1/4 cups unbleached all-purpose flour
1 teaspoon baking soda
1 teaspoon baking powder
1 1/2 cups fructose or table
  sugar (sucrose)
1/2 cup unsweetened applesauce

1 cup egg whites or liquid egg substitute
3/4 cup nonfat (skim) milk
1 teaspoon pure vanilla extract
1 tablespoon apple cider vinegar
1 cup chopped bananas
3/4 cup fresh or frozen blueberries

Preheat oven to 350F (175C). Spray 12 mini Bundt pans with vegetable oil spray. Into a small bowl, sift together flour, baking soda, and baking powder; set aside.

In a large bowl, beat fructose, applesauce, egg whites, milk, vanilla, and vinegar with an electric mixer until combined. Add flour mixture to applesauce mixture and beat until smooth. Fold in chopped bananas and blueberries.

Pour batter into prepared pans. Bake 30 to 35 minutes or until a wooden pick inserted into cake centers comes out clean. Cool cakes in pans 10 minutes, then turn out onto a wire rack to finish cooling.

KRYSTINE'S
HEALTHY
GOURMET
BAKERY
COOKBOOK

138

WHOLE-WHEAT CINNAMON CRUMB CAKE

Makes 10 servings

This wholesome dessert captures the richness of buttery coffeecake without all the fat. It has half the butter of a traditional recipe. I love to eat a slice of this for breakfast with a glass of ice-cold, freshly squeezed orange juice and a large mug of dark-roast coffee.

PER SERVING
Cal 277
Carb 46 gm
Prot 4 gm
Total fat 8 gm
Sat fat 1 gm
Cal from fat 26%
Chol 0 mg
Sodium 311 mg

Crumb Topping (see opposite)
3/4 cup unbleached all-purpose flour
3/4 cup whole-wheat flour
1/2 teaspoon salt
1 teaspoon baking soda
1 teaspoon ground cinnamon
4 tablespoons reduced-fat margarine
3/4 cup fructose or table sugar (sucrose)
1/4 cup egg whites or liquid egg substitute
3/4 cup water
1 teaspoon pure vanilla extract

CRUMB TOPPING
4 tablespoons reduced-fat margarine, chilled
1/2 cup unbleached all-purpose flour
1/2 cup maple syrup granules or granulated brown sugar
1 teaspoon ground cinnamon
1/4 cup rolled oats
1/2 cup chopped pecans

Preheat oven to 350F (175C). Spray a 9-inch-round cake pan with vegetable oil spray. Make topping: In a small bowl, combine topping ingredients and, using a pastry blender, mix until crumbly; set aside. In another small bowl, stir together flours, salt, baking soda, and cinnamon; set aside.

In a large bowl, beat margarine and fructose with an electric mixer until light and creamy. Add egg whites, water, and vanilla and beat until incorporated. Add flour mixture to butter mixture and beat until smooth.

Pour batter into prepared pan. Sprinkle topping evenly over batter. Bake 25 to 30 minutes or until a wooden pick inserted into center comes out clean. Cool in pan 10 minutes. Serve warm or turn out onto a wire rack to finish cooling.

BLACKBERRY UPSIDE-DOWN COFFEECAKE

Makes 10 servings

PER SERVING
Cal 356
Carb 55 gm
Prot 5 gm
Total fat 13 gm
Sat fat 9 gm
Cal from fat 33%
Chol 25 mg
Sodium 369 mg

After you experience this delectable white cake with its topping of deep purple blackberries, regular coffeecake will never taste the same again. Served at many of my brunches, this cake is one of those memorable desserts my friends still continue to talk about.

2 1/2 cups fresh or frozen blackberries
1 1/4 cups fructose or table sugar (sucrose)
2 cups cake flour
1 teaspoon baking powder
1 teaspoon baking soda
1/2 teaspoon salt

1/2 cup butter, softened
2/3 cup egg whites or liquid egg substitute
1 cup nonfat sour cream
2 tablespoons maple syrup granules or granulated brown sugar

Preheat oven to 350F (175C). Spray a 9-inch-round cake pan generously with vegetable oil spray. Pour blackberries and 1/4 cup of the fructose into pan and toss to combine. Spread evenly to completely cover bottom of pan; set aside.

Into a small bowl, sift together flour, baking powder, soda, and salt; set aside. In a large bowl, beat butter and remaining 1 cup fructose with an electric mixer until light and creamy. Add egg whites and sour cream and beat until smooth. Add flour mixture to butter mixture and beat until thoroughly combined, about 1 minute.

Pour batter over blackberries and spread evenly. Bake 35 to 40 minutes or until a wooden pick inserted into center comes out clean. Cool in pan 15 minutes, then remove cake from pan by turning upside down on a serving plate. Sprinkle with maple syrup granules while cake is still warm.

KRYSTINE'S
HEALTHY
GOURMET
BAKERY
COOKBOOK

140

CINNAMON, CHOCOLATE CHIP, YOGURT COFFEECAKE

Makes 14 servings

Auntie Dinah used chocolate and cinnamon—a sensational combination—to create this cake. I have altered it slightly by substituting fructose for regular sugar and replacing sour cream with nonfat yogurt. It is our family tradition to have this every Christmas morning; I look forward to this cake every year.

Filling/Topping (see opposite)
1/2 cup butter, softened
1 cup fructose or table sugar (sucrose)
1/2 cup liquid egg substitute
1 cup nonfat plain yogurt
1 teaspoon pure vanilla extract
2 cups cake flour
1 teaspoon baking powder
1 teaspoon baking soda

FILLING/TOPPING
1/2 cup maple syrup granules or
   granulated brown sugar
1 teaspoon ground cinnamon
1 cup chocolate chips
1/2 cup chopped walnuts (optional)

Preheat oven to 350F (175C). Butter and flour a 10-inch tube pan. Make filling/topping: In a medium bowl, mix together maple syrup granules, cinnamon, chocolate chips, and walnuts, if using; set aside.

In a large bowl, beat butter and fructose until light. Add egg substitute and mix well. Add yogurt and vanilla and beat until creamy. Sift flour, baking powder, and baking soda into yogurt mixture and stir until combined.

Pour half of the batter into prepared pan. Sprinkle with half of the filling mixture. Pour remaining batter over filling. Top with remaining filling mixture. Bake 50 to 60 minutes or until a wooden pick inserted into center comes out clean. Cool cake in pan 10 minutes, then turn out onto a wire rack to finish cooling.

NONFAT CINNAMON-APPLE COFFEECAKE

Makes 14 servings

This light and airy cake is superb! It tastes just like butter-rich coffeecake without the fat. Nonfat yogurt replaces the fat and calories of butter.

PER SERVING
Cal 161
Carb 34 gm
Prot 4 gm
Total fat 0.5 gm
Sat fat 0 gm
Cal from fat 3%
Chol 0 mg
Sodium 118 mg

Filling (see opposite)
2 cups unbleached all-purpose flour
1 teaspoon baking powder
1 teaspoon baking soda
1 1/2 cups nonfat plain yogurt
3/4 cup fructose or table sugar (sucrose)
1/2 cup liquid egg substitute or egg whites

FILLING
1/2 cup maple syrup granules or
    granulated brown sugar
3/4 cup diced Granny Smith apples
1 teaspoon ground cinnamon

Preheat oven to 350F (175C). Spray a 10-inch tube pan with vegetable oil spray. Make filling: In a small bowl, combine filling ingredients; set aside. Into a large bowl, sift together flour, baking powder, and baking soda; set aside.

In a medium bowl, beat yogurt, fructose, and egg substitute until combined. Add flour mixture to yogurt mixture and stir until combined; do not overbeat.

Pour half of batter into prepared pan. Sprinkle half of filling on top of batter. Pour remaining batter over filling and sprinkle remaining filling over batter. Bake 1 hour or until a wooden pick inserted into center comes out clean. Cool cake in pan 10 minutes, then turn out onto a wire rack to finish cooling.

KRYSTINE'S
HEALTHY
GOURMET
BAKERY
COOKBOOK

142

CHOCOLATE MACADAMIA COFFEECAKE

Makes 14 servings

My passion for great coffeecake has led me to combine buttery cake, chocolate, and macadamia nuts for the ultimate coffeecake. A best-seller at the bakery, it is perfect to serve with breakfast or brunch.

PER SERVING
Cal 380
Carb 58 gm
Prot 5 gm
Total fat 15 gm
Sat fat 5 gm
Cal from fat 35%
Chol 18 mg
Sodium 255 mg

Cinnamon Filling/Topping (see opposite)
1 3/4 cups unbleached all-purpose flour
1/4 cup unsweetened cocoa powder
1 teaspoon baking powder
1 teaspoon baking soda
1/2 teaspoon salt
1/2 cup butter, softened
3/4 cup fructose or table sugar (sucrose)
1/4 cup maple syrup granules or
    granulated brown sugar
1/2 cup egg whites or liquid egg substitute
1 cup nonfat plain yogurt
1 teaspoon pure vanilla extract
1/2 cup chocolate chips

CINNAMON FILLING/TOPPING
3/4 cup fructose or sugar
3/4 cup maple syrup granules or
    granulated brown sugar
1 1/2 tablespoons ground cinnamon
3/4 cup chopped macadamia nuts

Preheat oven to 350F (175C). Spray a 10-inch tube pan with vegetable oil spray. Make filling/topping: In a small bowl, combine all filling ingredients; set aside. Into another small bowl, sift together flour, cocoa, baking powder, baking soda, and salt; set aside.

In a large bowl, beat butter, fructose, and maple syrup granules with an electric mixer until light and creamy. Add egg whites, yogurt, and vanilla and beat well. Add flour mixture to yogurt mixture and mix until thoroughly combined. Fold in chocolate chips.

Pour half of batter into prepared pan. Sprinkle half of filling over batter. Pour remaining batter over filling, then sprinkle with remaining filling. Bake 1 hour or until a wooden pick inserted into center comes out clean. Cool cake in pan 10 minutes. Serve warm or turn out onto a wire rack to finish cooling.

WHOLE-WHEAT BANANA-SOUR CREAM COFFEECAKE

Makes 14 servings

PER SERVING
Cal 190
Carb 32 gm
Prot 2 gm
Total fat 6 gm
Sat fat 4 gm
Cal from fat 28%
Chol 12 mg
Sodium 173 mg

The goodness of whole wheat combined with sweet bananas and sour cream makes this a crowd pleaser.

1 cup unbleached all-purpose flour
1 cup whole-wheat flour
1 teaspoon baking powder
1 teaspoon baking soda
1/4 teaspoon salt

1/3 cup butter, softened
1 cup fructose or table sugar (sucrose)
1/4 cup mashed banana
1/2 cup nonfat sour cream

Preheat oven to 350F (175C). Spray a 10-inch tube pan with vegetable oil spray. In a small bowl, stir together flours, baking powder, baking soda, and salt; set aside.

In a large bowl, beat butter, fructose, banana, and sour cream with an electric mixer until creamy. Add flour mixture to banana mixture and stir until incorporated.

Pour batter into prepared pan. Bake 50 to 55 minutes or until a wooden pick inserted into center comes out clean. Cool cake in pan 10 minutes, then turn out onto a wire rack to finish cooling.

KRYSTINE'S
HEALTHY
GOURMET
BAKERY
COOKBOOK

144

SPECIALTY CAKES

This special chapter highlights the exclusive desserts made famous by the bakery. The recipes in this chapter consist of three different categories: cheesecakes, cake rolls, and celebrity bombes.

The cheesecake is considered an international dessert. Its origins go back as far as the Roman conquests, although the ones in this chapter only go back a few years. Our cheesecakes, specifically the White-Chocolate Raspberry Truffle, have helped make the bakery famous by their exposure on ABC's "Mike & Maty Show" and on the cover of this book. All recipes have had fat and calories reduced; however, even though the calories are fewer, these are not the desserts for everyday consumption. They should be reserved for special occasions.

Our cake rolls make my knees go weak. They consist of a dense, moist cake filled with a thick custard or cream center rolled up tightly into a decorative log. The cake roll has the special distinction of being our most well-traveled dessert. It all began when movie star Dennis Quaid began coming into the bakery for a slice of Low-Fat Pumpkin Cake Roll every morning when he was in town. One day, somewhat concerned, he informed me that he was leaving for the former Soviet-bloc country of Czechoslovakia (now known as Slovakia) to film on location, some 7,000 miles away. He was hoping it was possible to send him a Low-Fat Pumpkin Cake Roll when requested. I told him it wasn't a problem, and so for seven months, once a week, he would contact me and I would send him a roll. Now you can make them in your very own kitchen.

What is a Nonfat Chocolate Bombe? I didn't know either until this creation came to me in a dream: a nonfat mini Bundt cake drenched in nonfat frosting, smothered with nonfat cake crumbs, and topped with more nonfat frosting. This huge success is always in demand with our Hollywood patrons.

All specialty cakes are made with no egg yolks, and most cake rolls and all bombes have no added fat. I think you will be very pleased with this chapter. Have fun!

Cheesecake Tips

You will need a 9-inch springform pan, which will allow you to remove the cheesecake from the pan without flipping it over. You need only to remove the rim of the pan, leaving the cheesecake on the pan bottom.

Bring eggs and cream cheese to room temperature, making sure the cream cheese is completely softened before mixing. If not, it will change the entire integrity of the cheesecake and become lumpy when beaten, making your cake mushy and soggy.

KRYSTINE'S
HEALTHY
GOURMET
BAKERY
COOKBOOK

146

FRESH BANANA CUSTARD CAKE ROLL

Makes 12 servings

Rich-tasting Bavarian Custard fills this dense, moist banana cake. Customers find this cake to be phenomenal, and so will you.

1 recipe Bavarian Custard (page 187)
2 3/4 cups unbleached all-purpose flour
2 teaspoons baking soda
1/2 teaspoon salt
1/2 cup butter, softened

1 1/2 cups fructose or table sugar (sucrose)
2 1/2 cups mashed bananas
1 cup egg whites or liquid egg substitute
2/3 cup nonfat plain yogurt
2 teaspoons pure vanilla extract

PER SERVING
Cal 483
Carb 81 gm
Prot 11 gm
Total fat 12 gm
Sat fat 7 gm
Cal from fat 22%
Chol 32 mg
Sodium 434 mg

Prepare custard and refrigerate.

Preheat oven to 350F (175C). Spray a 17 × 12-inch jelly-roll pan with vegetable oil spray. Line bottom of pan with waxed paper; spray paper. Into a small bowl, sift together flour, baking soda, and salt; set aside.

In a large bowl, beat butter and fructose with an electric mixer until light and creamy. Add bananas, egg whites, yogurt, and vanilla and beat until smooth. Add flour mixture to banana mixture and beat until combined.

Pour batter into prepared pan. Bake 20 minutes or until a wooden pick inserted into center comes out clean. Let cake cool in pan 10 minutes on a wire rack.

Spread warm cake with custard. Begin rolling cake in pan, using the waxed-paper liner for support and peeling it away as you roll. Cool in refrigerator 1 hour before serving.

NONFAT CHOCOLATE CAKE ROLL

Makes 12 servings

PER SERVING
Cal 371
Carb 79 gm
Prot 10 gm
Total fat 0.5 gm
Sat fat 0 gm
Cal from fat 3%
Chol 0 mg
Sodium 269 mg

Marty Ingels and Shirley Jones have ordered this cake on more than one occasion. This delicious nonfat cake roll is filled with a chocolate filling that is also fat free! It is truly a winning combination. Make sure you prepare the filling ahead of time.

1 recipe Nonfat Chocolate Yogurt Filling (page 194)
1 1/2 cups unbleached all-purpose flour
1/2 cup unsweetened cocoa powder
2 teaspoons baking powder
1/2 teaspoon salt

1 1/2 cups egg whites or liquid egg substitute
2 cups fructose or table sugar (sucrose)
2/3 cup water
1 teaspoon pure vanilla extract

Prepare filling and refrigerate.

Preheat oven to 325F (165C). Spray a 17 × 12-inch jelly-roll pan with vegetable oil spray. Line bottom of pan with waxed paper; spray paper. Into a small bowl, sift together flour, cocoa, baking powder, and salt; set aside.

In a large bowl, beat egg whites, fructose, water, and vanilla with an electric mixer until light. Add flour mixture to egg mixture and beat until smooth and creamy.

Pour batter into prepared pan. Bake 20 minutes or until a wooden pick inserted in center comes out clean.

Let cake cool in pan 10 minutes on a wire rack. Spread warm cake with filling. Begin rolling cake in pan, using the waxed-paper liner for support and peeling it away as you roll. Cool in refrigerator 1 hour before serving.

KRYSTINE'S
HEALTHY
GOURMET
BAKERY
COOKBOOK

148

LOW-FAT PUMPKIN CAKE ROLL

Makes 12 to 14 servings

This is one of my best-known desserts. It has traveled all over the world. Dennis Quaid had me send this to him while filming the movie Dragon Heart *in Slovakia! This dessert is too good to be true! Serve with nonfat frozen vanilla yogurt, if desired.*

PER SERVING
Cal 559
Carb 117 gm
Prot 17 gm
Total fat 2 gm
Sat fat 0.5 gm
Cal from fat 4%
Chol 3 mg
Sodium 305 mg

Yogurt Cheese Filling (see opposite)
3 cups unbleached all-purpose flour
6 tablespoons pumpkin pie spice
4 teaspoons baking powder
2 2/3 cups egg substitute
2 2/3 cups canned pumpkin
3 cups fructose or table sugar (sucrose)

YOGURT CHEESE FILLING
1 1/2 recipes (3 cups) Nonfat Yogurt
   Cheese (page 192)
3/4 cup fructose or table sugar (sucrose)
2 teaspoons pure vanilla extract

Prepare filling: Combine filling ingredients in a medium bowl and refrigerate.

Preheat oven to 325F (165C). Spray 2 (17 × 12-inch) jelly-roll pans with vegetable oil spray. Line bottoms of pans with waxed paper; spray paper. Into a large bowl, sift together flour, pumpkin pie spice, and baking powder. Add egg substitute, pumpkin, and fructose and beat with an electric mixer until smooth.

Pour batter into prepared pans and spread evenly. Bake 20 to 25 minutes.

Let cake cool in pan 15 minutes on a wire rack. Spread 1 warm cake with three-quarters of the filling. Begin rolling cake in pan, using the waxed-paper liner for support and peeling it away as you roll.

Refrigerate rolled cake and remaining cake in refrigerator 1 hour or until completely cooled. Tear unrolled cake into pieces and put into a food processor; process into cake crumbs.

Spoon remaining filling over filled roll, rubbing over top and sides of roll so crumbs will adhere. With your hands, press crumbs firmly onto roll, covering roll completely. Serve within 4 hours.

LOW-FAT CARROT CAKE BOMBES

Makes 10 servings

PER SERVING
Cal 576
Carb 127 gm
Prot 14 gm
Total fat 1 gm
Sat fat 0 gm
Cal from fat 1%
Chol 0 mg
Sodium 303 mg

These beautiful cake balls look and taste sensational. You can buy these only at Krystine's Bakery; now you can make them yourself.

2 cups unbleached all-purpose flour
1 3/4 cups fructose or table sugar (sucrose)
1 teaspoon ground cinnamon
2 teaspoons baking soda
1 cup nonfat plain yogurt
3/4 cup liquid egg substitute
2/3 cup pureed cooked carrots or
    baby-food carrots
1/2 cup chopped fresh pineapple
1/2 cup golden raisins

FROSTING
4 cups nonfat plain yogurt
1 1/2 cups fructose or table sugar
    (sucrose)
3/4 cup pineapple juice

Preheat oven to 350F (175C). Spray 8 mini Bundt pans with vegetable oil spray. Into a small bowl, sift together flour, fructose, cinnamon, and baking soda; set aside.

In a large bowl, beat yogurt, egg substitute, and carrots with an electric mixer until combined. Add flour mixture to carrot mixture and beat until combined. Lightly stir in pineapple and raisins.

Pour batter into prepared pans. Bake 30 minutes or until a wooden pick inserted into cake centers comes out clean. Cool in pans 30 minutes, then cool completely on a wire rack.

Place 3 cakes in the freezer for 30 minutes or until cold but not frozen. Tear cakes into pieces. Add, one at a time, to a food processor and process into crumbs, about 40 seconds.

Make frosting: In a large bowl, combine yogurt, fructose, and juice. Dip remaining cakes, one at a time, into frosting to coat. Take a handful of cake crumbs and press firmly onto each cake until it is shaped like a softball. Spoon more frosting over top of each cake. Serve within 4 hours. Cut each cake in half before serving.

KRYSTINE'S
HEALTHY
GOURMET
BAKERY
COOKBOOK

150

NONFAT CHOCOLATE BOMBES

Makes 14 servings

A big, big seller at Krystine's Bakery and a celebrity favorite, these bombes will send you to chocolate euphoria! Decorate tops with fresh raspberries, if desired.

PER SERVING
Cal 378
Carb 84 gm
Prot 7 gm
Total fat 0.9 gm
Sat fat 0 gm
Cal from fat 2%
Chol 0 mg
Sodium 278 mg

4 cups unbleached all-purpose flour
1 1/2 cups fructose or table sugar (sucrose)
3/4 cup unsweetened cocoa powder
4 teaspoons baking soda
2 cups nonfat plain yogurt

2 cups water
2 tablespoons cider vinegar
1/2 cup egg whites or liquid egg substitute
1 recipe Nonfat Chocolate Frosting
  (page 183)

Preheat oven to 350F (175C). Spray 12 mini Bundt cake pans with vegetable oil spray. Into a medium bowl, sift together flour, fructose, cocoa, and baking soda; set aside. In another bowl, whisk together yogurt, water, vinegar, and egg whites. Add flour mixture to yogurt mixture and beat on medium speed for 3 minutes or until consistency is like pudding.

Pour batter into prepared pans. Bake 30 minutes or until a wooden pick inserted into cake centers comes out clean. Cool in pans 30 minutes, then cool completely on a wire rack.

Place 5 cakes in the freezer for 30 minutes or until cold but not frozen. Tear cakes into pieces. Add, one at a time, to a food processor and process into crumbs, about 40 seconds.

Make frosting and set aside. Dip remaining cakes, one at a time, into frosting to coat. Take a handful of cake crumbs and press firmly onto each cake until it is shaped like a softball. Spoon more frosting over top of each cake. Serve within 4 hours. Cut each cake in half before serving.

CHOCOLATE CHIP– COOKIE DOUGH CHEESECAKE

Makes 14 servings

PER SERVING
Cal 224
Carb 49 gm
Prot 7 gm
Total fat 5 gm
Sat fat 0 gm
Cal from fat 20%
Chol 17 mg
Sodium 185 mg

This is a wonderful cheesecake. The homemade cookie dough transforms this home run dessert into a grand slam.

1 Graham Cracker Crust (page 109), pressed onto bottom of a 9-inch springform pan
2 (8-ounce) packages light cream cheese, softened
1 (8-ounce) package nonfat cream cheese, softened
1 cup fructose or table sugar (sucrose)
1 egg
1/2 cup liquid egg substitute
1 cup nonfat plain yogurt

COOKIE DOUGH
1/4 cup reduced-fat margarine
1/4 cup maple syrup granules or granulated brown sugar
1/4 cup fructose or table sugar (sucrose)
1/2 cup unbleached all-purpose flour
2 tablespoons water
1 teaspoon pure vanilla extract
3/4 cup chocolate chips

Place crust in freezer while preparing filling.

Preheat oven to 300F (150C). In a large bowl, combine cream cheese and fructose and beat with an electric mixer until light and creamy. Add egg, egg substitute, and yogurt and beat 2 minutes. Pour filling into prepared crust; set aside.

Make cookie dough: In a small bowl, combine all ingredients and beat until thoroughly blended. Drop rounded tablespoonfuls of dough onto cheese filling and push dough down until it is covered with the cheese filling.

Bake 2 hours or until filling jiggles slightly when tapped. Cool in refrigerator at least 4 hours before removing pan rim.

KRYSTINE'S
HEALTHY
GOURMET
BAKERY
COOKBOOK

152

PEANUT BUTTERY–CHOCOLATE CHUNKY CHEESECAKE

Makes 14 servings

This decadent, fudgy, gooey sensation has been reduced in fat as much as possible, but it still weighs in as a dessert that you will probably want to save for a special treat. Decorate by chopping peanut-butter chocolate candy (sugar free if available) and sprinkling it generously on top of cake, if desired.

PER SERVING
Cal 421
Carb 73 gm
Prot 15 gm
Total fat 18 gm
Sat fat 1 gm
Cal from fat 38%
Chol 15 mg
Sodium 506 mg

1 Graham Cracker Crust (page 109), pressed onto bottom of a 9-inch springform pan
2 (8-ounce) packages light cream cheese, softened
2 (8-ounce) packages nonfat cream cheese, softened
3/4 cup fructose or table sugar (sucrose)
3/4 cup liquid egg substitute
1 cup nonfat plain yogurt
1 1/2 cups chocolate chips
1/2 cup reduced-fat creamy peanut butter
1/4 cup low-fat evaporated milk

Place crust in freezer while preparing filling.

Preheat oven to 300F (150C). In a large bowl, combine the light cream cheese, 1 package of the nonfat cream cheese, and fructose and beat with an electric mixer until well blended. Add egg substitute and yogurt and beat until smooth and creamy. Pour filling into prepared crust; set aside.

In a medium bowl, combine remaining nonfat cream cheese, 3/4 cup of the chocolate chips, and peanut butter and beat with an electric mixer until well blended. Drop rounded teaspoonfuls of peanut mixture onto cheese filling. Do not swirl. Bake 2 hours or until filling jiggles slightly when tapped.

In a small saucepan, melt remaining 3/4 cup chocolate chips with evaporated milk over low heat, stirring constantly, until smooth. Pour over cheesecake. Cool in refrigerator at least 4 hours before removing pan rim.

PUMPKIN CHEESECAKE

Makes 14 servings

PER SERVING
Cal 258
Carb 31 gm
Prot 8 gm
Total fat 12 gm
Sat fat 2 gm
Cal from fat 42%
Chol 20 mg
Sodium 255 mg

I love this cheesecake: the crunchy pecan crust provides a wonderful contrast in taste and texture to the smooth, creamy filling with its hint of spice. It's a big seller during the holidays, but I serve it any time of the year. Serve with fresh whipped cream, if desired.

Pecan Crust (see opposite)
1/2 cup liquid egg substitute
1 3/4 cups canned pumpkin
1/2 cup maple syrup granules or
   granulated brown sugar
1/2 teaspoon pure vanilla extract
2 teaspoons pumpkin pie spice
1 1/2 cups nonfat evaporated milk
2 (8-ounce) packages light cream cheese,
   softened
1/2 cup fructose or table sugar (sucrose)
2/3 cup nonfat plain yogurt

PECAN CRUST
1 1/4 cups finely crushed graham crackers
1/2 cup finely chopped pecans
2 tablespoons melted butter

Make crust: In a medium bowl, combine graham cracker crumbs, pecans, and melted butter. Press firmly onto bottom of a 9-inch springform pan. Place in freezer while preparing filling.

Preheat oven to 300F (150C). In a medium bowl, beat egg substitute, pumpkin, maple syrup granules, vanilla, pumpkin pie spice, and evaporated milk with an electric mixer until smooth, about 1 minute; set aside.

In a large bowl, combine cream cheese, fructose, and yogurt and beat until creamy, about 2 minutes. Stir pumpkin mixture into cream cheese mixture until thoroughly combined.

Pour filling into prepared crust. Bake 2 hours or until filling jiggles slightly when tapped. Cool in refrigerator at least 4 hours before removing pan rim.

KRYSTINE'S
HEALTHY
GOURMET
BAKERY
COOKBOOK

154

DAIRY-FREE, EGG-FREE, FRESH STRAWBERRY TOFU CHEESECAKE

Makes 14 servings

This cake actually makes you feel healthy as you're devouring it! Crunchy graham pecan crust is filled with a no-egg, no-dairy tofu filling. It's low in fat and high in protein. Decorate with plump ripe fresh strawberries.

Maple-Pecan Crust (see opposite)
2 tablespoons agar-agar flakes
2/3 cup soy milk
3/4 cup apple or orange juice concentrate
1/4 cup freshly squeezed lemon juice
2 teaspoons fresh lemon rind
2 teaspoons pure vanilla extract
2 1/2 cups mashed extra-firm tofu
2 cups fresh strawberries, hulled

MAPLE-PECAN CRUST
2 cups graham cracker crumbs
1 cup chopped pecans
1/4 cup soy margarine or butter, melted
1/2 cup pure maple syrup
1/2 teaspoon ground cinnamon

Make crust: In a medium bowl, combine graham cracker crumbs, pecans, margarine, maple syrup, and cinnamon. Press firmly onto bottom of a 9-inch springform pan. Place in freezer while preparing filling.

Preheat oven to 325F (165C). In a small saucepan, combine agar-agar flakes and soy milk. Let stand 5 minutes, then add fruit juice concentrate and simmer over low heat, stirring constantly, 5 minutes. Pour mixture into a food processor and add lemon juice, lemon rind, vanilla, and tofu. Process until smooth.

Pour tofu filling into prepared crust and spread evenly. Bake 10 to 15 minutes. Cool in refrigerator at least 4 hours before removing pan rim. Top with strawberries.

WHITE CHOCOLATE–RASPBERRY TRUFFLE CHEESECAKE

Makes 14 servings

After I made this cake on ABC's "Mike and Maty Show," the telephones at the bakery rang for weeks—everyone in America wanted this recipe. It is fantastic and tremendously reduced in fat.

PER SERVING
Cal 368
Carb 45 gm
Prot 12 gm
Total fat 16 gm
Sat fat 1 gm
Cal from fat 39%
Chol 27 mg
Sodium 483 mg

1 Graham Cracker Crust (page 109), pressed onto bottom of a 9-inch springform pan

2 (8-ounce) packages light cream cheese, softened

2 (8-ounce) packages nonfat cream cheese, softened

1 cup fructose or table sugar (sucrose)

3/4 cup liquid egg substitute

1 cup nonfat plain yogurt

1 1/2 cups vanilla or white chocolate chips

1/3 cup fruit-sweetened raspberry preserves

1/4 cup nonfat evaporated milk

Place crust in freezer while preparing filling.

Preheat oven to 300F (150C). In a large bowl, beat 3 packages of cream cheese and fructose with an electric mixer until well blended. Add egg substitute and yogurt and beat about 2 minutes. Pour filling into prepared crust; set aside.

In a medium bowl, beat remaining cream cheese, 3/4 cup of the vanilla chips, and raspberry preserves with an electric mixer until well blended. Drop rounded tablespoonfuls onto plain cheese filling. Do not swirl. Bake 1 hour and 40 minutes or until filling jiggles slightly when tapped.

Melt remaining 3/4 cup of white chips with evaporated milk over low heat, stirring constantly, until smooth; pour over cheesecake. Cool in refrigerator at least 2 hours before removing pan rim.

KRYSTINE'S
HEALTHY
GOURMET
BAKERY
COOKBOOK

156

LOW-FAT
NEW YORK
CHEESECAKE

Makes 14 servings

Quick and simple, this American original is a favorite at the bakery. It's great for any occasion, a hit with family and friends.

PER SERVING
Cal 259
Carb 74 gm
Prot 11 gm
Total fat 5 gm
Sat fat 0 gm
Cal from fat 17%
Chol 6 mg
Sodium 368 mg

1 Graham Cracker Crust (page 109), pressed onto bottom of a 9-inch springform pan
3 (8-ounce) packages nonfat cream cheese, softened
1 cup liquid egg substitute
3/4 cup fructose or table sugar (sucrose)
1 teaspoon freshly squeezed lemon juice
1 teaspoon pure vanilla extract

TOPPING
1 cup nonfat sour cream
1/3 cup fructose or table sugar (sucrose)

Place crust in freezer while preparing filling.

Preheat oven to 375F (190C). In a large bowl, beat cream cheese, egg substitute, fructose, lemon juice, and vanilla with an electric mixer until smooth and creamy.

Pour filling into prepared crust. Bake 40 minutes. Remove from oven and increase oven temperature to 450F (230C).

Make topping: In a small bowl, whisk sour cream and fructose until combined. Spread over cheesecake and bake 15 minutes more. Cool in refrigerator at least 4 hours before removing pan rim.

COCONUT-PINEAPPLE
TRUFFLE CHEESECAKE

Makes 14 servings

PER SERVING
Cal 213
Carb 47 gm
Prot 11 gm
Total fat 8 gm
Sat fat 1 gm
Cal from fat 34%
Chol 14 mg
Sodium 395 mg

Filled with sweet tropical pineapple "truffles" and the goodness of flaked coconut, this cheesecake is sinfully rich-tasting. The crust enhances the feel of an island paradise.

1 Macadamia Nut Crust (page 113), pressed onto bottom of a 9-inch springform pan

4 (8-ounce) packages light cream cheese, softened

3/4 cup fructose or table sugar (sucrose)

1/2 cup nonfat yogurt

1 cup liquid egg substitute

1 teaspoon pure vanilla extract

1/2 cup crushed pineapple, drained

TOPPING

1 egg white

1/3 cup fructose or sugar

2/3 cup sweetened flaked coconut, toasted (see Note, page 31)

Place crust in freezer while preparing filling.

Preheat oven to 325F (165C). In a large bowl, beat 3 packages of cream cheese and 1/2 cup of the fructose with an electric mixer until smooth. Add yogurt, egg substitute, and vanilla and beat until smooth and creamy. Pour filling into prepared crust; set aside.

In a small bowl, combine remaining package of cream cheese, remaining 1/4 cup fructose, and pineapple and beat until thoroughly combined. Drop rounded tablespoonfuls of pineapple mixture onto plain cheese filling. Do not swirl. Bake 45 minutes.

Make topping: In a bowl, beat egg white with an electric mixer until soft peaks form. Gradually beat in fructose until stiff peaks form. Fold in toasted coconut. Spread over cheesecake and bake 20 minutes more or until topping is browned. Cool in refrigerator at least 4 hours before removing pan rim.

KRYSTINE'S
HEALTHY
GOURMET
BAKERY
COOKBOOK

158

WHITE CHOCOLATE-LEMON CHEESECAKE

Makes 14 servings

This lemon-scented light and creamy cheesecake is a bakery best-seller. The combination of fresh lemon and white chocolate is a match made in heaven.

PER SERVING
Cal 277
Carb 39 gm
Prot 8 gm
Total fat 10 gm
Sat fat 1 gm
Cal from fat 32%
Chol 14 mg
Sodium 282 mg

1 Graham Cracker Crust (page 109), pressed onto bottom of a 9-inch springform pan
2 (8-ounce) packages light cream cheese, softened
1 cup fructose or table sugar (sucrose)

1 cup liquid egg substitute
1 tablespoon freshly grated lemon rind
1 tablespoon freshly squeezed lemon juice
1/2 cup nonfat lemon yogurt
1 cup vanilla or white chocolate chips, melted

Place crust in freezer while preparing filling.

Preheat oven to 350F (175C). In a large bowl, beat cream cheese, fructose, and egg substitute with an electric mixer until light and fluffy. Beat in lemon rind, lemon juice and yogurt until smooth. Stir in vanilla chips.

Pour filling into prepared crust. Bake 1 hour or until filling jiggles slightly when tapped. Cool in refrigerator at least 4 hours before removing pan rim.

LOW-FAT LEMON CHEESECAKE

Makes 14 servings

This wonderful no-fat cheesecake filling gets its super tangy flavor by using lemon-flavored yogurt, fresh lemon juice, and lemon rind.

PER SERVING
Cal 248
Carb 71 gm
Prot 11 gm
Total fat 4 gm
Sat fat 0 gm
Cal from fat 14%
Chol 6 mg
Sodium 370 mg

1 Graham Cracker Crust (page 109), pressed onto bottom of a 9-inch springform pan
3 (8-ounce) packages nonfat cream cheese, softened
3/4 cup liquid egg substitute
3/4 cup fructose or table sugar (sucrose)
3/4 cup nonfat lemon yogurt
1 tablespoon freshly grated lemon rind
1 tablespoon freshly squeezed lemon juice

TOPPING
1 cup nonfat sour cream
2 tablespoons fructose or table sugar (sucrose)
1 teaspoon pure vanilla extract

Place crust in freezer while preparing filling.

Preheat oven to 350F (175C). In a large bowl, beat cream cheese, egg substitute, and fructose with an electric mixer until light. Beat in yogurt, lemon rind, and lemon juice until smooth and creamy.

Pour filling into prepared crust. Bake 1 hour. Remove from oven and increase oven temperature to 450F (230C).

Make topping: In a small bowl, whisk sour cream, fructose, and vanilla until combined. Spread over cheesecake and bake 15 minutes more. Cool in refrigerator at least 6 hours before removing pan rim.

KRYSTINE'S
HEALTHY
GOURMET
BAKERY
COOKBOOK

160

FRESH BANANA CHEESECAKE
WITH MACADAMIA CRUST

Makes 14 servings

The filling of fresh banana pulp and cream cheese baked in a macadamia crust makes this very special dessert absolutely delicious.

PER SERVING
Cal 284
Carb 41 gm
Prot 8 gm
Total fat 9 gm
Sat fat 0 gm
Cal from fat 28%
Chol 15 mg
Sodium 299 mg

1 Macadamia Nut Crust (page 113), pressed onto bottom of a 9-inch springform pan
2 (8-ounce) packages light cream cheese, softened
1 cup mashed ripe bananas
2/3 cup fructose or table sugar (sucrose)
3/4 cup egg whites or liquid egg substitute
1 tablespoon freshly squeezed lemon juice
1/2 cup nonfat plain yogurt
1/2 cup low-fat evaporated milk
1 teaspoon pure vanilla extract

TOPPING
1 cup nonfat sour cream
2 tablespoons fructose or table sugar (sucrose)
1 teaspoon pure vanilla extract

Place crust in freezer while preparing filling.

Preheat oven to 325F (165). In a large bowl, beat cream cheese, bananas, fructose, and egg whites with an electric mixer until light and creamy. Beat in lemon juice, yogurt, evaporated milk, and vanilla until smooth.

Pour filling into prepared crust. Bake 55 minutes. Remove from oven and increase oven temperature to 375F (190C).

Make topping: In a small bowl, whisk sour cream, fructose, and vanilla until combined. Spread over cheesecake and bake 15 minutes more. Cool in refrigerator at least 6 hours before removing pan rim.

ESPRESSO-CHIP
CHEESECAKE

Makes 14 servings

PER SERVING
Cal 390
Carb 79 gm
Prot 11 gm
Total fat 14 gm
Sat fat 0 gm
Cal from fat 32%
Chol 11 mg
Sodium 365 mg

My mouth waters if I just look at this cheesecake. The pairing of chocolate and dark coffee is one of my favorite combinations.

1 Graham Cracker Crust (page 109), pressed onto bottom of a 9-inch springform pan

2 (8-ounce) packages nonfat cream cheese, softened

1 (8-ounce) package light cream cheese, softened

3/4 cup liquid egg substitute

1 cup fructose or table sugar (sucrose)

1 1/2 cups chocolate chips, melted

2 tablespoons instant coffee granules

1 teaspoon hot water

1 cup nonfat sour cream

3/4 cup chocolate chips

Place crust in freezer while preparing filling.

Preheat oven to 350F (175C). In a large bowl, beat cream cheese, egg substitute, and fructose with an electric mixer until light and fluffy. Stir in melted chocolate chips. Combine instant coffee and water in a small cup and add to cheese mixture. Whisk in sour cream and chocolate chips until thoroughly combined.

Pour filling into prepared crust. Bake 1 hour and 10 minutes or until cheesecake is firm. Cool in refrigerator at least 6 hours before removing pan rim.

KRYSTINE'S
HEALTHY
GOURMET
BAKERY
COOKBOOK

162

LOW-FAT CARROT CAKE CHEESECAKE

Makes 14 servings

This is our best-selling nonfat cheesecake filling. One bite and you'll know why. The flavor of creamy cheesecake and moist fruity carrot cake combined into one is truly magnificent.

PER SERVING
Cal 249
Carb 47 gm
Prot 6 gm
Total fat 2 gm
Sat fat 0 gm
Cal from fat 12%
Chol 0 mg
Sodium 122 mg

1 Graham Cracker Crust (page 109), pressed onto bottom of a 9-inch springform pan

CARROT-CAKE FILLING
1 cup unbleached all-purpose flour
3/4 cup fructose or table sugar (sucrose)
1 teaspoon ground cinnamon
1/2 cup nonfat cottage cheese
1/3 cup pureed cooked carrots or baby-food carrots

NONFAT CHEESE FILLING
1 (8-ounce) package nonfat cream cheese, softened
1/2 cup fructose or table sugar (sucrose)
1/3 cup egg whites or liquid egg substitute
1/2 cup nonfat plain yogurt

Place crust in freezer while preparing filling.

Preheat oven to 325F (165C). Make Carrot-Cake Filling: In a medium bowl, combine flour, fructose, cinnamon, cottage cheese, and carrot puree. Stir until thoroughly combined. Pour into prepared crust; set aside.

Make Nonfat Cheese Filling: In another medium bowl, beat cream cheese, fructose, egg whites, and yogurt with an electric mixer until light and creamy. Pour over carrot cake batter. Bake 45 to 50 minutes or until cake jiggles slightly when tapped. Cool in refrigerator at least 2 hours before removing pan rim.

FROSTINGS AND FILLINGS

A great frosting and/or filling can totally transform a plain, ordinary cake. No celebration cake is ever complete without the luxurious blanket of a creamy frosting or flavorful filling, which adds elegance and contrast in texture as well as delicious flavor. A beautifully decorated cake will undoubtedly be the focal point of any party.

Many of the frostings in this chapter call for a nonfat base consisting of skim milk and flour, which greatly reduces the amount of fat yet still yields a thick, creamy frosting. Instead of using one or two sticks of butter, you will need only half the amount that you would in a traditional buttercream. Other frostings are prepared with light cream cheese and nonfat milk. Fillings are prepared with nonfat milk or low-fat evaporated milk to cut down the fat.

I encourage you to experiment and have fun mixing and matching frostings and fillings with the various cakes in this book and with your own recipes.

Cook's Tip

You will need 2 cups of filling for a 2-layer cake, 2 to 3 cups of filling for a cake roll, and 3 to 4 cups of filling for a cream pie.

MAPLE COCONUT-PECAN FROSTING

Makes enough frosting for a 2-layer, 9-inch cake

The exciting combination of maple, coconut, and pecans makes the most incredible Old-Fashioned German Chocolate Cake (page 126). It's sensational over fudge brownies, too.

1 1/2 cups low-fat evaporated milk
1 cup maple syrup granules or
   granulated brown sugar
1 cup fructose or table sugar (sucrose)
1/3 cup reduced-fat margarine

3/4 cup liquid egg substitute
3/4 cup sweetened flaked coconut
2 teaspoons pure vanilla extract
3/4 cup pecans, chopped

In a medium saucepan, combine evaporated milk, maple syrup granules, fructose, and margarine. Cook over low heat, stirring constantly, until mixture comes to a boil. Remove pan from heat and whisk in egg substitute. Cook over low heat, stirring constantly, until mixture returns to a boil. Remove from heat and stir in coconut, vanilla, and pecans. Chill in refrigerator at least 90 minutes before using.

KRYSTINE'S
HEALTHY
GOURMET
BAKERY
COOKBOOK

166

JUICE-SWEETENED
CREAM CHEESE FROSTING

Makes enough frosting for a 2-layer, 9-inch cake

Sweetened only with fruit juice, this frosting is a wonderful replacement when generously spread on carrot, apple, and banana cake. The fruit juice adds a wonderfully fresh, clean flavor.

1/12 OF RECIPE
Cal 153
Carb 12 gm
Prot 6 gm
Total fat 10 gm
Sat fat 0 gm
Cal from fat 58%
Chol 20 mg
Sodium 320 mg

3 (8-ounce) packages light cream cheese, softened
3/4 cup frozen pineapple juice concentrate, thawed

1 teaspoon pure vanilla extract
1 teaspoon freshly grated lemon rind

In a medium bowl, beat all ingredients with an electric mixer until light and fluffy. Chill in refrigerator at least 90 minutes before using.

PINEAPPLE CREAM CHEESE FROSTING

Makes enough frosting for a 2-layer, 9-inch cake

This exciting combination of pineapple and cream cheese tastes fabulous on Maui Pineapple Cake (see page 124) or carrot cake.

1/3 cup unbleached all-purpose flour
1 cup nonfat (skim) milk
3/4 cup frozen pineapple juice
  concentrate, thawed

1/2 cup (4 ounces) light cream cheese
1 tablespoon freshly grated lemon rind
1 teaspoon pure vanilla extract

In a small saucepan, whisk together flour and milk. Cook over medium heat, stirring constantly, until mixture is a thick paste, 2 to 3 minutes. Remove from heat and cool in refrigerator at least 1 hour.

In a medium bowl, combine pineapple juice concentrate, cream cheese, lemon rind, vanilla, and cooled paste and beat with an electric mixer until smooth. Chill in refrigerator at least 90 minutes before using.

KRYSTINE'S
HEALTHY
GOURMET
BAKERY
COOKBOOK

168

CHOCOLATE WALNUT ICING

Makes enough frosting for a 2-layer, 9-inch cake

The ultimate of all chocolate icings is a perfect complement to any of our brownies, especially Blue-Ribbon Fudgy Brownies (page 60).

1/2 cup butter or margarine
1 1/2 cups fructose or table sugar (sucrose)
1/3 cup low-fat evaporated milk

1/2 cup chocolate chips
2 teaspoons pure vanilla extract
1 cup chopped walnuts

1/12 OF RECIPE
Cal 295
Carb 37 gm
Prot 2 gm
Total fat 16 gm
Sat fat 5 gm
Cal from fat 49%
Chol 22 mg
Sodium 87 mg

In a medium saucepan, combine butter, fructose, and milk. Bring to a boil over low heat, stirring constantly. Boil 1 minute without stirring. Remove from heat and stir in chocolate chips until completely melted. Stir in vanilla and walnuts. Chill in refrigerator at least 90 minutes before using.

LOW-FAT
CREAM CHEESE
FROSTING

Makes enough frosting for a 2-layer, 9-inch cake

This rich and creamy frosting is an excellent alternative to the traditional standard for carrot cake.

1/12 OF RECIPE
Cal 101
Carb 19 gm
Prot 2 gm
Total fat 2 gm
Sat fat 0 gm
Cal from fat 16%
Chol 4 mg
Sodium 64 mg

1/3 cup unbleached all-purpose flour
1 cup nonfat (skim) milk
3/4 cup fructose or table sugar (sucrose)

1/2 cup (4 ounces) light cream cheese, softened
1 teaspoon pure vanilla extract

In a small saucepan, whisk flour and milk. Cook over medium heat, stirring constantly, until mixture is a thick paste, 2 to 3 minutes. Remove from heat and cool in refrigerator at least 1 hour.

In a medium bowl, combine fructose, cream cheese, vanilla, and cooled paste and beat with an electric mixer until smooth. Chill in refrigerator at least 90 minutes before using.

KRYSTINE'S
HEALTHY
GOURMET
BAKERY
COOKBOOK

170

CITRUS CREAM CHEESE
FROSTING

Makes enough frosting for a 2-layer, 9-inch cake

*Orange and lemon rind scent this luxurious cream cheese most beautifully—
a must atop carrot or lemon cake.*

1/12 OF RECIPE
Cal 102
Carb 20 gm
Prot 2 gm
Total fat 2 gm
Sat fat 0 gm
Cal from fat 17%
Chol 3 mg
Sodium 57 mg

1/3 cup unbleached all-purpose flour
1 cup nonfat (skim) milk
3/4 cup fructose or table sugar (sucrose)
1/2 cup (4 ounces) light cream cheese,
   softened

1/4 cup frozen orange juice concentrate
1 teaspoon freshly grated lemon rind
1 tablespoon freshly grated orange rind

In a small saucepan, whisk together flour and milk. Cook over medium heat, stirring constantly, until mixture is a thick paste, 2 to 3 minutes. Remove from heat and cool in refrigerator at least 1 hour.

In a medium bowl, combine fructose, cream cheese, juice concentrate, lemon rind, orange rind, and cooled paste and beat with an electric mixer until smooth. Chill in refrigerator at least 90 minutes before using.

WHITE CHOCOLATE-
CREAM CHEESE FROSTING

Makes enough frosting for a 2-layer, 9-inch cake

This luxurious frosting complements just about any cake.

1/2 cup vanilla or white chocolate chips, melted and cooled

1 1/2 cups (12 ounces) light cream cheese, softened

1/2 cup butter, softened

1 cup fructose or table sugar (sucrose)

1 teaspoon pure vanilla extract

1 teaspoon freshly squeezed lemon juice

In a medium bowl, combine melted chocolate chips, cream cheese, butter, fructose, vanilla, and lemon juice. Beat with an electric mixer until smooth and creamy. Chill in refrigerator at least 90 minutes before using.

KRYSTINE'S
HEALTHY
GOURMET
BAKERY
COOKBOOK

172

MAPLE BUTTERCREAM FROSTING

Makes enough frosting for a 2-layer, 9-inch cake

With its deep, rich maple flavor, this creamy, easy-to-work-with frosting is a perfect complement to apple or spice cake.

1/3 cup unbleached all-purpose flour
1 cup nonfat (skim) milk
1/2 cup butter, softened

3/4 cup pure maple syrup
1 teaspoon pure vanilla extract

1/12 OF RECIPE
Cal 144
Carb 18 gm
Prot 1 gm
Total fat 8 gm
Sat fat 5 gm
Cal from fat 48%
Chol 21 mg
Sodium 109 mg

In a small saucepan, whisk together flour and milk. Cook over medium heat, stirring constantly, until mixture is a thick paste, 2 to 3 minutes. Remove from heat and cool in refrigerator at least 1 hour.

In a medium bowl, combine butter, maple syrup, vanilla, and cooled paste and beat with an electric mixer until smooth and creamy. Chill in refrigerator at least 90 minutes before using.

LEMON-VANILLA FROSTING

Makes enough frosting for a 2-layer, 9-inch cake

1/12 OF RECIPE
Cal 191
Carb 29 gm
Prot 1 gm
Total fat 8 gm
Sat fat 5 gm
Cal from fat 37%
Chol 21 mg
Sodium 89 mg

The essence of fresh lemon makes this unbelievably delicious on top of lemon, chocolate, or yellow cake.

1/3 cup unbleached all-purpose flour
1 cup nonfat (skim) milk
1/2 cup butter, softened
1 1/4 cups fructose

1/4 cup freshly squeezed lemon juice
2 tablespoons freshly grated lemon rind
2 teaspoons pure vanilla extract

In a small saucepan, whisk together flour and milk. Cook over medium heat, stirring constantly, until mixture is a thick paste, 2 to 3 minutes. Remove from heat and cool in refrigerator at least 1 hour.

In a medium bowl, combine butter, fructose, lemon juice, lemon rind, vanilla, and cooled paste and beat with an electric mixer until smooth and creamy. Chill in refrigerator at least 90 minutes before using.

KRYSTINE'S
HEALTHY
GOURMET
BAKERY
COOKBOOK
174

VANILLA BUTTERCREAM FROSTING

Makes enough frosting for a 2-layer, 9-inch cake

The subtle combination of vanilla and buttercream makes this a versatile frosting that can be used with all cakes.

1/3 cup unbleached all-purpose flour
1 cup nonfat (skim) milk
1/2 cup butter, softened

1 cup fructose or table sugar (sucrose)
2 teaspoons pure vanilla extract

1/12 OF RECIPE
Cal 170
Carb 24 gm
Prot 1 gm
Total fat 8 gm
Sat fat 5 gm
Cal from fat 41%
Chol 21 mg
Sodium 88 mg

In a small saucepan, whisk together flour and milk. Cook over medium heat, stirring constantly, until mixture is a thick paste, 2 to 3 minutes. Remove from heat and cool in refrigerator at least 1 hour.

In a medium bowl, combine butter, fructose, vanilla, and cooled paste and beat with an electric mixer until smooth and creamy. Chill in refrigerator at least 90 minutes before using.

WHITE CHOCOLATE FROSTING

Makes enough frosting for a 2-layer, 9-inch cake

*Mellow and creamy, this frosting is magnificent with chocolate
or lemon cake.*

1/12 OF RECIPE
Cal 109
Carb 13 gm
Prot 2 gm
Total fat 6 gm
Sat fat 4 gm
Cal from fat 48%
Chol 16 mg
Sodium 74 mg

1/3 cup unbleached all-purpose flour
1 cup nonfat (skim) milk
1 cup vanilla or white chocolate chips

1/3 cup butter, softened
1/3 cup fructose or table sugar (sucrose)
1 teaspoon pure vanilla extract

In a small saucepan, whisk together flour and milk. Cook over medium heat, stirring constantly, until mixture is a thick paste, 2 to 3 minutes. Remove from heat and cool in refrigerator at least 1 hour.

After paste has cooled, melt vanilla chips in top of a double boiler over simmering water; set melted chips aside to cool. In a medium bowl, combine butter, fructose, vanilla, melted chips, and cooled paste and beat with an electric mixer until smooth and creamy. Chill in refrigerator at least 90 minutes before using.

KRYSTINE'S
HEALTHY
GOURMET
BAKERY
COOKBOOK

176

MILK CHOCOLATE FROSTING

Makes enough frosting for a 2-layer, 9-inch cake

This silky, creamy, decadent frosting is glorious on brownies, chocolate cake, or yellow cake. It also is a perfect companion for just about any cupcake.

1/3 cup unbleached all-purpose flour
1 1/4 cups nonfat (skim) milk

1 1/2 cups milk chocolate chips
2 teaspoons pure vanilla extract

1/12 OF RECIPE
Cal 50
Carb 7 gm
Prot 2 gm
Total fat 1 gm
Sat fat 0 gm
Cal from fat 20%
Chol 4 mg
Sodium 32 mg

In a small saucepan, whisk together flour and 1 cup of the milk. Cook over medium heat, stirring constantly, until mixture is a thick paste, 2 to 3 minutes. Remove from heat and cool in refrigerator at least 1 hour.

After paste has cooled, melt chocolate chips and remaining 1/4 cup milk in another small saucepan over low heat; set melted chips aside to cool.

In a medium bowl, combine vanilla, melted chips, and cooled paste and beat with an electric mixer until smooth and creamy. Chill in refrigerator at least 90 minutes before using.

MOCHA FROSTING

Makes enough frosting for a 2-layer, 9-inch cake

The coffee and chocolate flavors in this buttercream frosting are remarkably intense.

1/12 OF RECIPE
Cal 170
Carb 24 gm
Prot 1 gm
Total fat 8 gm
Sat fat 5 gm
Cal from fat 41%
Chol 21 mg
Sodium 88 mg

1/3 cup unbleached all-purpose flour
3/4 cup nonfat (skim) milk
1/3 cup strong coffee
1/2 cup butter, softened

1/4 cup unsweetened cocoa powder
1 cup fructose or table sugar (sucrose)
2 teaspoons pure vanilla extract

In a small saucepan, whisk together flour and milk. Cook over medium heat, stirring constantly, until mixture is a thick paste, 2 to 3 minutes. Remove from heat and cool in refrigerator at least 1 hour.

In a medium bowl, combine coffee, butter, cocoa, fructose, vanilla, and cooled paste and beat with an electric mixer until smooth and creamy. Chill in refrigerator at least 90 minutes before using.

KRYSTINE'S
HEALTHY
GOURMET
BAKERY
COOKBOOK

178

TOFU-CHEESE FROSTING

Makes enough frosting for a 2-layer, 9-inch cake

This smooth and creamy frosting smothered all over carrot cake tastes outstanding and makes you feel healthier with every bite.

1/3 cup unbleached all-purpose flour
1 cup nonfat (skim) milk or soy milk
1/2 cup pureed tofu (pureed in food processor or blender)

1/2 cup (4 ounces) light cream cheese, softened
1/2 cup fructose or table sugar (sucrose)
2 teaspoons pure vanilla extract

1/12 OF RECIPE
Cal 90
Carb 15 gm
Prot 3 gm
Total fat 2 gm
Sat fat 0 gm
Cal from fat 21%
Chol 4 mg
Sodium 65 mg

In a small saucepan, whisk together flour and milk. Cook over medium heat, stirring constantly, until mixture is a thick paste, 2 to 3 minutes. Remove from heat and cool in refrigerator at least 1 hour.

In a medium bowl, combine tofu, cream cheese, fructose, vanilla, and cooled paste and beat with an electric mixer until smooth and creamy. Chill in refrigerator at least 90 minutes before using.

CHOCOLATE TOFU FROSTING

Makes enough frosting for a 2-layer, 9-inch cake

Accessorize your cakes with this deliciously, chocolatey, smooth-as-silk frosting

1/3 cup unbleached all-purpose flour
1 cup nonfat (skim) milk or soy milk
1 1/2 cups chocolate chips
1/2 cup pureed tofu (pureed in food processor or blender)

2 teaspoons pure vanilla extract
1/4 cup pure maple syrup

In a small saucepan, whisk together flour and milk. Cook over medium heat, stirring constantly, until mixture is a thick paste, 2 to 3 minutes. Remove from heat and cool in refrigerator at least 1 hour.

After paste has cooled, melt chocolate chips in a double boiler over simmering water, stirring constantly, until smooth; set melted chips aside to cool.

In a medium bowl, combine melted chips, tofu, vanilla, maple syrup, and cooled paste and beat with an electric mixer until smooth and creamy. Chill in refrigerator at least 90 minutes before using.

KRYSTINE'S
HEALTHY
GOURMET
BAKERY
COOKBOOK

180

FLUFFY WHITE FROSTING

Makes enough frosting for a 2-layer, 9-inch cake

A family favorite, this one brings back happy memories of how I couldn't wait to lick the beaters (sometimes even while they were still running). A versatile frosting for all kinds of cakes, it's perfect for birthdays and any special occasion.

1/12 OF RECIPE
Cal 150
Carb 18 gm
Prot 1 gm
Total fat 8 gm
Sat fat 5 gm
Cal from fat 47%
Chol 21 mg
Sodium 88 mg

5 tablespoons unbleached all-purpose flour
1 cup nonfat (skim) milk
1/2 cup butter, softened

3/4 cup fructose or table sugar (sucrose)
1 teaspoon pure vanilla extract

In a small saucepan, whisk together flour and milk. Cook over medium heat, stirring constantly, until mixture is a thick paste, 2 to 3 minutes. Remove from heat and cool in refrigerator at least 1 hour.

In a medium bowl, combine butter, fructose, vanilla, and cooled paste and beat with an electric mixer until smooth and creamy. Chill in refrigerator at least 90 minutes before using.

ORANGE BUTTERCREAM FROSTING

Makes enough frosting for a 2-layer, 9-inch cake

1/12 OF RECIPE
Cal 107
Carb 19 gm
Prot 2 gm
Total fat 5 gm
Sat fat 3 gm
Cal from fat 42%
Chol 15 mg
Sodium 110 mg

A perfect accompaniment to Fresh Orange Juice Cupcakes (page 134) or Orange-Scented Angel Food Cake (page 118).

5 tablespoons unbleached all-purpose flour
3/4 cup nonfat (skim) milk
1/2 cup (4 ounces) nonfat cream cheese
1/3 cup butter, softened
1/2 cup frozen orange juice concentrate, thawed

1/4 cup fructose or table sugar (sucrose)
1 tablespoon freshly grated orange rind
1 teaspoon pure vanilla extract

In a small saucepan, whisk together flour and milk. Cook over medium heat, stirring constantly, until mixture is a thick paste. Remove from heat and cool in refrigerator at least 1 hour.

In a medium bowl, combine cream cheese, butter, orange juice concentrate, fructose, orange rind, vanilla, and cooled paste and beat with an electric mixer until smooth and creamy. Chill in refrigerator at least 90 minutes before using.

KRYSTINE'S
HEALTHY
GOURMET
BAKERY
COOKBOOK

182

NONFAT CHOCOLATE FROSTING

Makes enough frosting for a 1-layer, 9-inch cake

This frosting is very smooth, almost puddinglike. It goes with just about any type of cake.

1/8 OF RECIPE
Cal 202
Carb 50 gm
Prot 0 gm
Total fat 0 gm
Sat fat 0 gm
Cal from fat 0%
Chol 0 mg
Sodium 0 mg

1/3 cup cornstarch

1/3 cup unsweetened cocoa powder

1 1/2 cups fructose or table sugar (sucrose)

3 cups water

Into a medium saucepan, sift together cornstarch, cocoa, and fructose. Pour in water and whisk thoroughly. Cook over low heat, whisking occasionally, until thickened, about 40 minutes. Use frosting while still warm.

NONFAT FLUFFY VANILLA FROSTING

Makes enough frosting for a 1-layer, 9-inch cake

Try this wonderful frosting on banana or yellow cake. Of course, I prefer it right off the beaters.

4 egg whites

1 1/2 cups fructose or table sugar (sucrose)

1/4 teaspoon cream of tartar

2 teaspoons pure vanilla extract

In the top of a double boiler, combine all ingredients. Cook over low heat, beating constantly with an electric mixer, until stiff peaks form, 7 minutes. Use immediately.

KRYSTINE'S
HEALTHY
GOURMET
BAKERY
COOKBOOK

184

LEMON LOVE NOTE GLAZE

Makes enough glaze for a 1-layer, 9-inch cake or tube cake

Featured on our lemon muffins (page 32), this tart, sweet glaze adds a nice touch to many different desserts. Try on scones or carrot cake.

1/8 OF RECIPE
Cal 128
Carb 33 gm
Prot 0 gm
Total fat 0 gm
Sat fat 0 gm
Cal from fat 0%
Chol 0 mg
Sodium 0 mg

1 cup fructose or powdered sugar
1 cup freshly squeezed lemon juice

2 teaspoons freshly grated lemon rind

In a medium bowl, whisk all ingredients until thoroughly combined.

CITRUS GLAZE

Makes enough glaze for a 1-layer, 9-inch cake or tube cake

Spread this on cinnamon rolls, Bundt cakes, or scones.
It has many different uses.

1/8 OF RECIPE
Cal 133
Carb 34 gm
Prot 0 gm
Total fat 0 gm
Sat fat 0 gm
Cal from fat 0%
Chol 0 mg
Sodium 0 mg

1 cup fructose or powdered sugar
1/2 cup freshly squeezed lemon juice

1/2 cup freshly squeezed orange juice
1/4 cup freshly squeezed lime juice

In a medium bowl, whisk all ingredients until thoroughly combined.

KRYSTINE'S
HEALTHY
GOURMET
BAKERY
COOKBOOK
186

BAVARIAN CUSTARD

Makes 3 cups

This fabulous reduced-fat custard can be used as a filling for just about any cake. I highly recommend it in the Fresh Banana Custard Cake Roll (page 147) or Nonfat Chocolate Cake Roll (page 148)

PER 1/4 CUP
Cal 89
Carb 9 gm
Prot 3 gm
Total fat 4 gm
Sat fat 2 gm
Cal from fat 41%
Chol 11 mg
Sodium 82 mg

1 1/2 cups nonfat (skim) milk

1/4 cup fructose or table sugar (sucrose)

1/4 cup butter

1/4 cup cornstarch

3/4 cup liquid egg substitute

1 teaspoon pure vanilla extract

In a large saucepan, combine 1 cup of the milk, fructose, and butter. Cook over low heat, stirring constantly, until mixture comes to a boil. Remove from heat.

In a small bowl, combine remaining 1/2 cup milk and cornstarch, whisking until cornstarch dissolves. Add egg substitute and cornstarch mixture to hot milk mixture. Cook over low heat, stirring constantly, until mixture comes to a boil. Remove from heat and stir in vanilla. Cool in refrigerator at least 2 hours before using.

NONFAT VANILLA YOGURT FILLING

Makes 2 1/2 cups

PER 1/4 CUP
Cal 153
Carb 32 gm
Prot 6 gm
Total fat 0 gm
Sat fat 0 gm
Cal from fat 0%
Chol 2 mg
Sodium 75 mg

This filling is very simple to make. You need to start the yogurt cheese the day before you plan to make your cake, because it needs 24 hours to drain and thicken. It's well worth the wait!

1 recipe Nonfat Yogurt Cheese
  (see page 192)

1 cup fructose or table sugar (sucrose)
2 teaspoons pure vanilla extract

In a medium bowl, mix yogurt cheese, fructose, and vanilla until light and creamy. Chill in refrigerator at least 90 minutes before using.

KRYSTINE'S
HEALTHY
GOURMET
BAKERY
COOKBOOK

188

COCONUT CREAM FILLING

Makes 4 cups

This filling is sensational! The coconut and vanilla custard are marvelous together. Serve it between layers of Coconut Custard Cake (see page 127) or a plain yellow cake (see page 119) and you'll have people raving over your dessert.

PER 1/4 CUP
Cal 102
Carb 16 gm
Prot 3 gm
Total fat 3 gm
Sat fat 2 gm
Cal from fat 25%
Chol 3 mg
Sodium 92 mg

3/4 cup fructose or table sugar (sucrose)
3 tablespoons cornstarch
1/4 teaspoon salt
2 cups nonfat (skim) milk

1 1/4 cups liquid egg substitute
1 tablespoon butter
3/4 cup sweetened flaked coconut
2 teaspoons pure vanilla extract

In a medium saucepan, whisk fructose, cornstarch, and salt thoroughly. Add milk and cook over low heat, stirring constantly, until mixture comes to a boil.

Remove from heat and whisk in egg substitute and butter. Cook over low heat, stirring constantly, until mixture comes to a boil. Remove from heat and stir in coconut and vanilla. Cool in refrigerator at least 2 hours before using.

COFFEE BRÛLÉE FILLING

Makes 2 cups

With a jolt of java, it's a perfect filling for chocolate cake.

PER 1/4 CUP
Cal 116
Carb 20 gm
Prot 5 gm
Total fat 1 gm
Sat fat 0 gm
Cal from fat 8%
Chol 1 mg
Sodium 80 mg

1/2 cup fructose or table sugar (sucrose)
3 tablespoons cornstarch
1/2 cup very strong coffee

1 1/2 cups nonfat (skim) milk
1 cup liquid egg substitute
1 teaspoon pure vanilla extract

In a medium saucepan, combine sugar and cornstarch, then slowly whisk in coffee and milk. Cook over medium heat, stirring constantly, until mixture comes to a boil.

Remove from heat and whisk in egg substitute. Cook over low heat, stirring constantly, 1 minute. Remove from heat and stir in vanilla. Chill in refrigerator at least 2 hours before using.

KRYSTINE'S
HEALTHY
GOURMET
BAKERY
COOKBOOK

190

LUSCIOUS LEMON FILLING

Very light and refreshing, what could be better than this tart citrus filling for a cake served at a summer picnic?

1 1/2 cups fructose or table sugar (sucrose)
3 tablespoons cornstarch
3 tablespoons unbleached all-purpose flour
Dash of salt
1 1/2 cups hot water

1 cup liquid egg substitute
3 egg yolks, beaten
2 tablespoons butter
1 teaspoon freshly grated lemon rind
1/3 cup freshly squeezed lemon juice

PER 1/4 CUP
Cal 139
Carb 26 gm
Prot 3 gm
Total fat 3 gm
Sat fat 1 gm
Cal from fat 20%
Chol 44 mg
Sodium 700 mg

In a medium saucepan, whisk together fructose, cornstarch, flour, and salt, then whisk in hot water. Cook over medium heat, stirring constantly, until mixture comes to a boil. Cook, stirring constantly, 2 minutes more.

Remove from heat and whisk in egg yolks. Cook over low heat, stirring constantly, until mixture boils 2 minutes.

Remove from heat and add butter, lemon rind, and lemon juice. Cool in refrigerator at least 90 minutes before using.

NONFAT YOGURT CHEESE

Makes 2 cups

This recipe is one of the very few in this book that must be prepared in advance. Use the yogurt cheese for cheesecakes, frostings, and fillings as a terrific fat alternative.

PER 1/4 CUP
Cal 68
Carb 9 gm
Prot 7 gm
Total fat 0 gm
Sat fat 0 gm
Cal from fat 0%
Chol 2 mg
Sodium 93 mg

4 cups nonfat plain yogurt without stabilizers

Line a large strainer with either flat coffee filters or cheesecloth. Pour in yogurt and place strainer in a large bowl or pan to catch yogurt drippings. Refrigerate at least 12 hours or up to 24 hours or until mixture is very thick. The yogurt cheese will keep in the refrigerator up to 2 weeks.

KRYSTINE'S
HEALTHY
GOURMET
BAKERY
COOKBOOK

192

NONFAT FRESH
STRAWBERRY CREAM FILLING

Makes 4 1/2 cups

A refreshing filling that goes well with any yellow or lemon cake. Try it in Fresh Banana Custard Cake Roll (page 147)—wow!

PER 1/4 CUP
Cal 105
Carb 24 gm
Prot 1 gm
Total fat 0 gm
Sat fat 0 gm
Cal from fat 0%
Chol 0 mg
Sodium 36 mg

2 cups nonfat sour cream

2 2/3 cups fresh strawberries, hulled

1 1/3 cups fructose or table sugar (sucrose)

1 teaspoon pure vanilla extract

In a food processor or blender, combine sour cream, strawberries, fructose, and vanilla. Process until smooth and creamy. Chill in refrigerator at least 90 minutes before using.

VARIATION
Substitute thawed and well-drained frozen unsweetened strawberries for fresh strawberries.

NONFAT CHOCOLATE
YOGURT FILLING

Makes 3 cups

*Created especially for the Nonfat Chocolate Cake Roll (page 148), but it
also goes well in any cake.*

PER 1/4 CUP
Cal 134
Carb 27 gm
Prot 5 gm
Total fat 0 gm
Sat fat 0 gm
Cal from fat 0%
Chol 2 mg
Sodium 70 mg

2 cups Nonfat Yogurt Cheese (page 192)   1 cup fructose or table sugar (sucrose)
1/4 cup nonfat dried milk powder   2 tablespoons strong coffee
1/2 cup unsweetened cocoa powder   1 teaspoon pure vanilla extract

In a medium bowl, whisk together yogurt cheese, dried milk, cocoa, fructose, coffee,
and vanilla and beat until smooth and creamy. Chill in refrigerator at least 90 minutes
before using.

KRYSTINE'S
HEALTHY
GOURMET
BAKERY
COOKBOOK

194

NONFAT BANANA CREAM FILLING

Makes 3 cups

Thick and creamy with fresh bananas in every bite, it is perfect for making a banana cream pie or for filling a cake.

1/2 cup fructose or table sugar (sucrose)
1/4 cup cornstarch
1 teaspoon unbleached all-purpose flour
2 1/2 cups nonfat (skim) milk

1/3 cup liquid egg substitute
2 teaspoons pure vanilla extract
2 medium bananas, sliced

PER 1/4 CUP
Cal 95
Carb 20 gm
Prot 3 gm
Total fat 0 gm
Sat fat 0 gm
Cal from fat 0%
Chol 11 mg
Sodium 39 mg

In a large saucepan, whisk together fructose, cornstarch, and flour. Stir in milk. Cook over medium heat, stirring constantly, until mixture boils and thickens, about 5 minutes.

Remove from heat and whisk in egg substitute. Cook over low heat, stirring constantly, until slightly thickened. Remove from heat and stir in vanilla extract and sliced bananas. Chill in refrigerator 2 hours before using.

DIABETIC RECIPES

This chapter is dedicated to a special group of people—diabetics. Diabetes mellitus is a life-long disease in which the pancreas does not produce enough insulin or our bodies do not use the insulin efficiently enough to properly process the foods that we eat.

I come from two generations of diabetics—both on my mother's and father's side. My grandmother Ethyl, who helped raise me as a child and taught me everything she knew about baking, died from this disease. Had she been more aware of the proper diet and taken her insulin, this tragedy could have been prevented. On the other hand, my great-grandmother Chizu, who is also diabetic, is thriving and able to manage her disease quite easily just by watching her diet. At the pristine age of eighty she still runs circles around me and takes care of my children.

During my years at the bakery, I have encountered many of my diabetic customers, literally in tears, because they could not find fresh-baked, good-quality desserts without sugar. Feeling their frustrations I created these recipes especially for them. The recipes fall into one of two categories: completely sweetened with fruit pulp and/or aspartame (Nutrasweet® brand sweetener) or with a fraction of the sugar called for in a traditional recipe. It is amazing how sweet and delicious something can still be without all the added sugar found in most desserts.

Diabetic Tip

When trying any new sweetener or changing your diet, always consult your physician first.

CINNAMON ROLLS

Makes 16 rolls

PER ROLL
Cal 163
Carb 33 gm
Prot 5 gm
Total fat 1 gm
Sat fat 0 gm
Cal from fat 3%
Chol 0 mg
Sodium 28 mg

This special version of almost sugar-free cinnamon rolls—they contain only 2 1/2 teaspoons of fructose, which is necessary for activating yeast—is spectacular. To make them even more delicious, top with Sugar-Free Glaze (opposite page).

3 tablespoons active dry yeast
2 1/2 teaspoons fructose
1 cup warm water
1/2 cup nonfat plain yogurt
3/4 cup liquid egg substitute
4 cups unbleached all-purpose flour
Filling (see opposite)
Sugar-Free Glaze (opposite page)

FILLING
3/4 cup raisins
2 tablespoons unsweetened applesauce
1 1/2 teaspoons ground cinnamon
2 tablespoons frozen apple juice
    concentrate, thawed

In a large bowl, dissolve yeast and fructose in warm water. Add yogurt and egg substitute and whisk until thoroughly combined. Using your hands, mix in flour to make a soft dough. Knead dough on a lightly floured board 10 minutes or until smooth and elastic.

Place kneaded dough in a lightly oiled bowl. Cover with plastic wrap and let the dough rise until doubled in size, about 1 hour.

Meanwhile, make filling: In a small bowl, combine all filling ingredients; set aside.

Using your fist, punch down the dough and knead 10 times. With a rolling pin, roll out the dough to a 1/4-inch-thick rectangle. Spread filling over dough, leaving a 1-inch border, and roll up tightly, jelly-roll style. Seal ends by pinching them together. Cut roll crosswise into 16 slices, about 1 1/2 inches wide.

Spray a nonstick baking sheet with vegetable oil spray. Place rolls, cut side down, on prepared baking sheet. Cover and let rise until doubled in size, about 30 minutes.

Preheat oven to 350F (175C). Bake 25 minutes or until lightly browned. Brush with glaze while rolls are still warm.

KRYSTINE'S
HEALTHY
GOURMET
BAKERY
COOKBOOK

198

SUGAR-FREE GLAZE

Makes enough glaze for 16 pastries

Delicious on cinnamon rolls, muffins, or tea breads, it adds that extra touch of sweetness most sugar-free desserts can use.

1 cup cold water
2 tablespoons cornstarch
2 teaspoons Equal (Nutrasweet®)

1 teaspoon freshly grated lemon rind
1 teaspoon pure vanilla extract

PER RECIPE
Cal 16
Carb 4 gm
Prot 0 gm
Total fat 0 gm
Sat fat 0 gm
Cal from fat 0%
Chol 0 mg
Sodium 1 mg

In a small saucepan, combine water and cornstarch and whisk until cornstarch is completely dissolved. Cook over low heat, stirring constantly, until mixture thickens, about 3 minutes. Remove from heat and stir in Equal, lemon rind, and vanilla.

BLUEBERRY-OAT BRAN MUFFINS

Makes 12 muffins

The aroma of fresh blueberries does wonders for my spirit! This delicious blueberry-filled bran muffin is sweetened with orange juice and 1/4 cup of fructose to make it lower in sugar than a regular muffin.

PER MUFFIN
Cal 158
Carb 26 gm
Prot 3 gm
Total fat 5 gm
Sat fat 1 gm
Cal from fat 28%
Chol 0 mg
Sodium 120 mg

1 cup unbleached all-purpose flour
2 1/2 teaspoons baking powder
1/4 cup vegetable oil
1/3 cup liquid egg substitute or egg whites
1/2 cup mashed ripe banana
2 tablespoons freshly grated orange rind

1/2 cup frozen orange juice concentrate, thawed
1 cup bran flakes cereal
1/2 cup oat bran
1/4 cup fructose
1 cup fresh or frozen blueberries

Preheat oven to 325F (165C). Spray 12 muffin cups with vegetable oil spray. Into a small bowl, sift together flour and baking powder; set aside.

In a large bowl, beat oil, egg substitute, banana, orange rind, orange juice concentrate, bran flakes, oat bran, and fructose with an electric mixer until incorporated. Add flour mixture to bran mixture and beat until combined. Gently stir in blueberries.

Spoon into prepared cups. Bake 25 minutes or until a wooden pick inserted into muffin centers comes out clean. Turn out muffins onto a wire rack to cool.

KRYSTINE'S
HEALTHY
GOURMET
BAKERY
COOKBOOK

200

LOW-SUGAR
BLUEBERRY-ORANGE
MUFFINS

Makes 12 muffins

Plump blueberries are surrounded by freshly squeezed orange juice cake. This muffin is low in sugar, reduced in fat, yet high in flavor.

PER MUFFIN
Cal 190
Carb 28 gm
Prot 4 gm
Total fat 7 gm
Sat fat 4 gm
Cal from fat 33%
Chol 18 mg
Sodium 111 mg

1 1/2 cups fresh or frozen blueberries
2 cups plus 2 tablespoons unbleached all-purpose flour
4 teaspoons baking powder
1/3 cup fructose
1/3 cup butter, softened

1/4 cup egg whites or liquid egg substitute
1/2 cup freshly squeezed orange juice
1/2 cup nonfat (skim) milk
1 teaspoon pure vanilla extract
1 tablespoon freshly grated orange rind

Preheat oven to 375F (190C). Spray 12 muffin cups with vegetable oil spray. In a small bowl, toss blueberries with the 2 tablespoons flour. Into a medium bowl, sift together flour and baking powder; set aside.

In a large bowl, beat fructose, butter, egg whites, orange juice, milk, vanilla, and orange rind with an electric mixer until light and creamy. Add flour mixture to butter mixture and beat until thoroughly combined, about 1 minute. Stir in blueberries.

Spoon batter into prepared muffin cups. Bake 25 minutes or until a wooden pick inserted into muffin centers comes out clean. Turn out muffins onto a wire rack to cool.

ZUCCHINI-PINEAPPLE BREAD

Makes 2 loaves; 20 slices

PER SLICE
Cal 120
Carb 15 gm
Prot 2 gm
Total fat 5 gm
Sat fat 1 gm
Cal from fat 37%
Chol 0 mg
Sodium 107 mg

A low-sugar quick bread, it is filled with pineapple and zucchini. If wrapped tightly, you can keep it in the freezer up to three months.

1 1/2 cups unbleached all-purpose flour
1 teaspoon baking powder
1/2 teaspoon baking soda
1/2 teaspoon salt
1 teaspoon ground cinnamon
1/2 cup canola oil
3/4 cup egg whites or liquid egg substitute

1/3 cup fructose
1 teaspoon pure vanilla extract
1/2 cup frozen pineapple juice concentrate, thawed
1 cup grated zucchini
1/2 cup canned crushed pineapple, drained

Preheat oven to 350F (175C). Spray 2 (9 × 5-inch) loaf pans with vegetable oil spray. Into a small bowl, sift together flour, baking powder, baking soda, salt, and cinnamon; set aside.

In a large bowl, beat oil, egg whites, fructose, vanilla, and pineapple juice concentrate until incorporated. Add flour mixture to egg white mixture and stir until blended. Fold in zucchini and pineapple.

Pour batter into prepared pans. Bake 40 to 45 minutes or until a wooden pick inserted into centers comes clean. Cool in pans 10 minutes. Turn breads out onto a wire rack to finish cooling. Cut into slices.

KRYSTINE'S
HEALTHY
GOURMET
BAKERY
COOKBOOK

202

ORANGE DATE BREAD

Makes 2 loaves; 20 slices

This low-sugar, high-fiber bread is a refreshing alternative to other quick breads. It's great toasted with your favorite spread, and hearty enough to eat just by itself.

PER SLICE
Cal 190
Carb 31 gm
Prot 3 gm
Total fat 6 gm
Sat fat 1 gm
Cal from fat 28%
Chol 0 mg
Sodium 65 mg

3 1/2 cups unbleached all-purpose flour
1/2 teaspoon baking soda
2 teaspoons baking powder
1 teaspoon cornstarch
1/3 cup fructose
1/2 cup liquid egg substitute

3/4 cup frozen orange juice concentrate, thawed
1/3 cup vegetable oil
2 tablespoons freshly grated orange rind
3/4 cup chopped dates
1/2 cup chopped pecans

Preheat oven to 350F (175C). Spray 2 (9 × 5-inch) loaf pans with vegetable oil spray. Into a small bowl, sift together flour, baking powder, baking soda, and cornstarch; set aside.

In a medium bowl, beat fructose, egg substitute, orange juice concentrate, oil, and orange rind until smooth. Add flour mixture to orange mixture and stir until incorporated. Fold in dates and pecans.

Pour batter into prepared pans. Bake 50 to 60 minutes or until a wooden pick inserted into centers comes clean. Cool in pans 10 minutes. Turn breads out onto a wire rack to finish cooling. Cut into slices.

SUGAR-FREE,
NONFAT STRAWBERRY-BANANA
SCONES

Makes 24 scones

PER SCONE
Cal 68
Carb 14 gm
Prot 2 gm
Total fat 0.3 gm
Sat fat 0 gm
Cal from fat 3%
Chol 0 mg
Sodium 230 mg

Freshly squeezed orange juice and banana pulp naturally sweeten these exceptionally delicious scones.

2 1/4 cups unbleached all-purpose flour
2 tablespoons baking powder
1/4 teaspoon salt
1/4 cup mashed ripe banana
1/4 cup nonfat plain yogurt
1/3 cup liquid egg substitute

1/2 cup freshly squeezed orange juice
1/4 cup nonfat (skim) milk
1/2 cup fresh or frozen strawberries, chopped
1/2 cup chopped banana

Preheat oven to 400F (205C). Spray a baking sheet with vegetable oil spray. Into a large bowl, sift together flour, baking powder, and salt. Add mashed banana, yogurt, egg substitute, orange juice, and milk. With your hands, combine mixture until thoroughly incorporated. Add strawberries and chopped banana and gently mix until evenly combined.

Using an ice cream scoop, drop the batter in mounds onto prepared baking sheet. Bake 20 to 25 minutes or until lightly browned. Serve warm.

KRYSTINE'S
HEALTHY
GOURMET
BAKERY
COOKBOOK

204

LOW-SUGAR, NONFAT APPLE-RAISIN SCONES

Makes 20 scones

Sweetened with applesauce, apple juice, and aspartame, these scones have no added fat and are rated our number-one-selling diabetic dessert.

2 cups unbleached all-purpose flour
1 1/2 tablespoons baking powder
1/4 teaspoon salt
1/4 cup unsweetened applesauce
1/4 nonfat plain yogurt
1/3 cup liquid egg substitute
1/2 cup nonfat (skim) milk
1/4 cup unsweetened apple juice
1/2 cup raisins
3/4 cup peeled, diced Granny Smith apples

GLAZE
1/4 cup apple juice
1 teaspoon cornstarch
1/4 teaspoon Equal (Nutrasweet®)

PER SCONE
Cal 68
Carb 15 gm
Prot 2 gm
Total fat 0.2 gm
Sat fat 0 gm
Cal from fat 2%
Chol 0 mg
Sodium 58 mg

Preheat oven to 400F (205C). Spray a baking sheet with vegetable oil spray. Into a large bowl, sift together flour, baking powder, and salt. Add yogurt, egg substitute, milk, apple juice, raisins, and apples. With your hands, combine mixture until thoroughly incorporated. Knead in bowl 2 minutes.

Using an ice cream scoop, drop the batter onto prepared baking sheet. Bake 20 to 25 minutes or until lightly browned.

While scones are baking, make glaze: In a small bowl, stir together apple juice, cornstarch, and Equal. Spoon glaze over warm scones.

PEACH STREUSEL BARS

Makes 12 bars

An enticing low-sugar treat, these bars have a buttery oatmeal crust filled with fruit-sweetened preserves, then covered with more oatmeal streusel topping. Simply fantastic!

PER BAR
Cal 257
Carb 33 gm
Prot 3 gm
Total fat 12 gm
Sat fat 7 gm
Cal from fat 42%
Chol 31 mg
Sodium 212 mg

1 1/2 cups unbleached all-purpose flour
1 1/2 cups rolled oats
1/3 cup fructose
1 teaspoon baking powder

1 teaspoon ground nutmeg
1/4 teaspoon salt
3/4 cup butter, chilled
1 cup fruit-sweetened peach preserves

Preheat oven to 375F (190C). In a large bowl, combine flour, oats, fructose, baking powder, nutmeg, and salt; mix thoroughly. Cut in butter with a pastry blender until mixture is crumbly. Reserve 1 cup of oat mixture for topping; set aside.

Press remaining oat mixture onto bottom of an ungreased 8-inch-square baking pan. Bake 10 minutes. Remove from oven and spread preserves over crust. Sprinkle reserved oat mixture over preserves; pat down gently. Bake 30 minutes or until golden brown. Cool in pan on a wire rack. Cut into bars.

KRYSTINE'S
HEALTHY
GOURMET
BAKERY
COOKBOOK

206

PINEAPPLE-MACADAMIA BARS

Makes 16 servings

These tropical fruit bars have a buttery crust and are primarily sweetened with fresh fruit, pineapple juice, and brown sugar. They are sweet and satisfying yet low in sugar.

PER SERVING
Cal 141
Carb 12 gm
Prot 3 gm
Total fat 9 gm
Sat fat 4 gm
Cal from fat 57%
Chol 16 mg
Sodium 88 mg

1 1/3 cups unbleached all-purpose flour
1/2 cup butter, softened
2 tablespoons pineapple juice
1 cup canned crushed pineapple, drained
1/4 cup maple syrup granules or
   granulated brown sugar

2/3 cup liquid egg substitute
1/2 teaspoon baking powder
1/2 cup chopped macadamia nuts

Preheat oven to 350F (175C). Spray a 9-inch-round cake pan with vegetable oil spray. In a medium bowl, combine flour, butter, and pineapple juice with a pastry blender until thoroughly blended. Press mixture onto bottom of prepared pan to make a crust. Bake 20 minutes and remove from oven.

While crust is baking, stir together pineapple, maple syrup granules, egg substitute, baking powder, and nuts until combined. Pour over crust. Bake 25 minutes. Cool in pan 10 minutes and cut into wedges.

LOW-FAT APPLE BREAD PUDDING

Makes 8 servings

PER SERVING
Cal 202
Carb 37 gm
Prot 10 gm
Total fat 1 gm
Sat fat 0 gm
Cal from fat 4%
Chol 2 mg
Sodium 200 mg

Fresh apples and applesauce add sweetness to this pudding. Serve warm with fresh whipped cream sweetened with Nutrasweet®, if desired.

1 1/2 cups nonfat evaporated milk
1/2 cup frozen apple juice concentrate, thawed
1 cup liquid egg substitute
1/3 cup unsweetened applesauce
2 teaspoons pure vanilla extract
1/2 teaspoon ground mace
1/2 teaspoon ground cinnamon
1/2 teaspoon ground nutmeg
4 cups (1/2-inch cubes) French or white bread
2 cups sliced Granny Smith apples
1/3 cup raisins

GLAZE
2 tablespoons hot water
4 teaspoons Equal (Nutrasweet®)

In a large bowl, whisk milk, apple juice concentrate, egg substitute, applesauce, vanilla, mace, cinnamon, and nutmeg until combined. Stir in bread cubes, apples, and raisins. Stir lightly until bread is saturated. Refrigerate 2 hours, stirring occasionally.

Preheat oven to 350F (175C). Spray an 8-inch-square baking dish with vegetable oil spray.

Pour bread mixture into prepared baking dish. Add 1/2 inch hot water to a baking pan large enough to hold baking dish. Place baking dish with bread pudding in water. Bake 50 minutes or until golden in color.

While pudding is baking, make glaze: In a small bowl, combine water and Equal. Spread glaze on pudding while it is still hot. Cool 30 minutes before serving.

KRYSTINE'S
HEALTHY
GOURMET
BAKERY
COOKBOOK

208

LOW-FAT CAROB MOUSSE

Makes 4 servings

Carob in place of chocolate gives you the chocolate taste without the caffeine. This recipe is sweetened with white grape juice in place of sugar. I like to serve it in a graham cracker crust and top it with sugar-free whipped cream.

PER SERVING
Cal 216
Carb 35 gm
Prot 18 gm
Total fat 2 gm
Sat fat 0 gm
Cal from fat 8%
Chol 3 mg
Sodium 181 mg

6 tablespoons carob powder

2 packages unflavored gelatin

1 cup liquid egg substitute

2 cups white grape juice (not concentrate)

2 tablespoons pure vanilla extract

5 packets Equal (Nutrasweet®)

2/3 cup nonfat dried milk powder

1/4 cup ice water

In a large saucepan, combine carob powder and gelatin. Mix in egg substitute and grape juice and whisk until all lumps are dissolved. Cook over low heat, stirring constantly, until mixture boils and thickens. Remove from heat and stir in vanilla and Equal.

Beat dry milk and ice water until stiff peaks form. Add carob mixture and beat until combined. Spoon into dessert glasses. Chill in refrigerator until set, about 1 hour.

BANANA-CHOCOLATE
CHUNK CAKE

Makes 12 servings

PER SERVING
Cal 409
Carb 54 gm
Prot 11 gm
Total fat 18 gm
Sat fat 6 gm
Cal from fat 40%
Chol 28 mg
Sodium 373 mg

It is such a pleasure to be able to find sugar-free chocolate candy. The chunks of chocolate in this supermoist banana cake make it marvelous. Top it with Sugar-Free Espresso Buttercream Frosting (page 215) and you'll think you've had a taste of heaven.

3 cups unbleached all-purpose flour
1 teaspoon cornstarch
1 teaspoon baking soda
1/2 cup butter, softened
1/3 cup fructose
3 cups mashed ripe bananas
1/2 cup sugar-free chocolate, broken into small pieces, or chocolate chips

1 cup liquid egg substitute
3/4 cup nonfat plain yogurt
Sugar-Free Espresso Buttercream Frosting (page 215)
2 tablespoons unsweetened cocoa powder

Preheat oven to 350F (175C). Spray 2 (8-inch-round) cake pans with vegetable oil spray. Into a small bowl, sift together flour, cornstarch, and baking soda; set aside.

In a large bowl, beat butter and fructose with an electric mixer until light, about 1 minute. Add bananas, chocolate pieces, egg substitute, and yogurt and beat until combined. Add flour mixture to banana mixture and beat 1 minute.

Pour batter into prepared cake pans. Bake 30 to 40 minutes or until a wooden pick inserted in cake centers comes out clean. Cool cakes in pans 10 minutes, then turn out onto a wire rack to finish cooling. Frost and fill with frosting. Sift a very thin coat of cocoa over cake.

KRYSTINE'S
HEALTHY
GOURMET
BAKERY
COOKBOOK

210

MALT-SWEETENED NONFAT CHOCOLATE DEVASTATION CAKE

Makes 12 servings

This barley malt–sweetened cake is not as sweet as the original devastation cake (page 133), but it is very good. Frost with your choice of sugar-free frosting.

PER SERVING
WITHOUT
FROSTING
Cal 128
Carb 25 gm
Prot 4 gm
Total fat 1 gm
Sat fat 0 gm
Cal from fat 7%
Chol 3 mg
Sodium 176 mg

2 cups cake flour
1/3 cup unsweetened cocoa powder
1/3 cup fructose
3/4 cup natural malted milk powder
2 teaspoons baking soda

1 cup nonfat plain yogurt
1/2 cup water
1 tablespoon apple cider vinegar
1 tablespoon pure vanilla extract
1/4 cup egg substitute

Preheat oven to 350F. Generously spray 2 (9-inch-round) cake pans with vegetable oil spray. Into a medium bowl, sift together flour, cocoa, fructose, malt powder, and baking soda; set aside.

In a large bowl, whisk yogurt, water, vinegar, vanilla, and egg substitute until blended. Add flour mixture to yogurt mixture and beat with an electric mixer until smooth, 3 minutes.

Pour batter into prepared cake pans. Bake 25 to 35 minutes or until a wooden pick inserted into cake centers comes out clean. Cool cakes in pans 10 minutes, then turn out onto a wire rack to finish cooling.

24-KARAT CAKE

Makes 12 servings

You'll certainly enjoy this scrumptious dessert sweetened with fruit juice concentrate. Fresh, ripe pineapple is always best, though you may use pineapple that is canned in juice if you wish.

PER SERVING
Cal 278
Carb 32 gm
Prot 9 gm
Total fat 13 gm
Sat fat 1 gm
Cal from fat 42%
Chol 13 mg
Sodium 346 mg

2 cups unbleached all-purpose flour
1 teaspoon baking powder
1 teaspoon baking soda
1 1/2 teaspoons ground cinnamon
1/3 cup safflower oil
2/3 cup canned pumpkin
3/4 cup liquid egg substitute
1/2 cup frozen apple juice concentrate, thawed

2/3 cup pureed, cooked carrots or baby-food carrots
2/3 chopped fresh pineapple
1/2 cup golden raisins
1 cup chopped walnuts (optional)
2/3 recipe Juice-Sweetened Cream Cheese Frosting (page 167)

Preheat oven to 350F (175C). Spray 2 (8-inch-round) cake pans with vegetable oil spray. Into a large bowl, sift together flour, baking powder, baking soda, and cinnamon. Add oil, applesauce, egg substitute, and apple juice concentrate and mix well. Stir in carrots, pineapple, raisins, and walnuts.

Pour batter into prepared pans. Bake 30 to 40 minutes or until a wooden pick inserted into cake centers comes out clean. Cool cakes in pans 10 minutes, then turn out onto a wire rack to finish cooling. Fill and frost cooled cake.

KRYSTINE'S
HEALTHY
GOURMET
BAKERY
COOKBOOK

212

NO-SUGAR-ADDED
VANILLA CHEESECAKE

Makes 12 servings

I created this magnificent treat especially for my diabetic grandmother.
Serve it with fresh berries.

PER SERVING
Cal 229
Carb 18 gm
Prot 10 gm
Total fat 13 gm
Sat fat 1 gm
Cal from fat 51%
Chol 25 mg
Sodium 382 mg

1 1/2 cups finely crushed fruit-sweetened
    graham crackers
2 tablespoons butter, melted
3 (8-ounce) packages light cream cheese,
    softened

2 tablespoons Nutrasweet® Spoonful™
3/4 cup liquid egg substitute or
    egg whites
1 cup nonfat plain yogurt
1 teaspoon lemon extract

In a medium bowl, combine graham cracker crumbs and melted butter. Press onto bottom of a 9-inch springform pan. Place in freezer while preparing filling.

Preheat oven to 300F (150C). In a medium bowl, beat cream cheese and Nutrasweet with an electric mixer until well blended. Add egg substitute, yogurt, and lemon extract and beat about 2 minutes.

Pour filling into prepared crust. Bake 1 hour and 40 minutes or until set. Chill before serving.

STRAWBERRY
CUSTARD ROLL

Makes 12 servings

Strawberry sponge cake surrounds sugar-free custard. With whipped cream and fresh strawberries on the side, you'll have your guests begging for seconds.

PER SERVING
Cal 227
Carb 25 gm
Prot 9 gm
Total fat 9 gm
Sat fat 5 gm
Cal from fat 35%
Chol 22 mg
Sodium 236 mg

2 cups unbleached all-purpose flour
2 teaspoons baking powder
1/3 cup fructose
1 2/3 cups strawberry pulp (2 1/2 cups
   strawberries and 1/2 cup water
   pureed in food processor)

1 1/3 cups liquid egg substitute
1 recipe sugar-free custard filling
   (page 217)

Preheat oven to 350F (175C). Spray a 17 × 12-inch jelly-roll pan with vegetable oil spray. Line bottom of pan with waxed paper; spray paper. Into a small bowl, sift together flour and baking powder; set aside.

In a large bowl, beat fructose, strawberry pulp, and egg substitute with an electric mixer until combined. Add flour mixture to strawberry mixture and beat 1 minute.

Spread cake batter in prepared pan. Bake 15 to 20 minutes or until cake springs back when touched.

Let cake cool in pan 10 minutes on a wire rack. Spread warm cake with custard. Begin rolling cake in pan, using the waxed-paper liner for support and peeling it away as you roll. Cool in refrigerator 2 hours before serving.

KRYSTINE'S
HEALTHY
GOURMET
BAKERY
COOKBOOK

214

SUGAR-FREE ESPRESSO BUTTERCREAM FROSTING

Makes enough frosting for a 2-layer, 9-inch cake

This is a very versatile frosting that can go with any chocolate cake, or if you like, try it on brownies.

1/12 OF RECIPE
Cal 86
Carb 6 gm
Prot 3 gm
Total fat 6 gm
Sat fat 0 .5 gm
Cal from fat 61%
Chol 7 mg
Sodium 180 mg

1/3 cup unbleached all-purpose flour
1 cup nonfat (skim) milk
1/3 cup reduced-fat margarine
1 (8-ounce) package light cream cheese, softened

1/2 cup espresso or very strong coffee
1 teaspoon pure vanilla extract
2 tablespoons nonfat (skim) milk
1/2 cup Nutrasweet® Spoonful™

In a small saucepan, whisk together flour and milk. Cook over medium heat, stirring constantly, until mixture is a thick paste, 2 to 3 minutes. Remove from heat and cool in refrigerator at least 1 hour.

In a medium bowl, combine margarine, cream cheese, coffee, vanilla, milk, Nutrasweet, and cooled paste and beat with an electric mixer until smooth. Chill in refrigerator at least 90 minutes before using.

NONFAT SUGAR-FREE
CHOCOLATE FROSTING

Makes enough frosting for a 2-layer, 9-inch cake

This is the same recipe that's on page 183 except I've substituted Nutrasweet® for the fructose. It tastes sweet and chocolatey, yet it's lower in carbohydrates for diabetics.

3/4 cup cornstarch

3/4 cup unsweetened cocoa powder

1/2 cup Nutrasweet® Spoonful™

6 cups water

Into a large saucepan, sift together cornstarch, cocoa, and Nutrasweet®. Add water and whisk until cocoa dissolves. Cook over medium heat, stirring constantly, until mixture thickens 20 to 30 minutes. Use while frosting is still hot.

KRYSTINE'S
HEALTHY
GOURMET
BAKERY
COOKBOOK

216

FRESH FRUIT,
SUGAR-FREE
CUSTARD TART

Makes 10 servings

A fabulous custard fills this tart. The choice of fruit is yours. I prefer many different fruits such as kiwi, peaches, blueberries, raspberries, and strawberries for taste and color.

PER SERVING
Cal 245
Carb 18 gm
Prot 10 gm
Total fat 14 gm
Sat fat 8 gm
Cal from fat 51%
Chol 35 mg
Sodium 252 mg

2 3/4 cups nonfat (skim) milk
1/2 cup butter
1/8 cup cornstarch
2/3 cup liquid egg substitute
1 teaspoon pure vanilla extract

1/4 cup Nutrasweet® Spoonful™
1 (10-inch) Standard Pie Crust,
(page 115), baked in a tart pan
Fresh fruit, for garnish

In a large saucepan, combine 2 1/2 cups of the milk and butter. Cook over low heat, stirring constantly, until milk comes to a boil; remove from heat.

In a small bowl, dissolve cornstarch in remaining 1/4 cup milk and stir in egg substitute. Stir cornstarch mixture into hot milk. Cook over low heat, stirring constantly, just until mixture bubbles, about 5 minutes.

Remove pan from heat and stir in Nutrasweet®. Pour into a bowl and refrigerate at least 3 hours. Pour into prepared tart crust. Garnish generously with fresh colorful fruit of the season.

APPLE-SWEETENED
APPLE-CRANBERRY COOKIES

Makes 24 servings

Sweetened mostly with applesauce, these cookies have all the taste without all the sugar. My son gobbled them up without realizing they were low in sugar.

1 1/2 cups unbleached all-purpose flour
1/2 teaspoon baking soda
1 teaspoon ground cinnamon
3/4 cup unsalted butter, softened
1/3 cup fructose
3/4 cup unsweetened applesauce
1/4 cup frozen apple juice concentrate, thawed

1/4 cup liquid egg substitute
1 teaspoon pure vanilla extract
1 3/4 cups unsweetened granola
3/4 cup diced dried apples
1/2 cup dried cranberries or raisins

Preheat oven to 325F (165C). Into a small bowl, sift together flour, baking soda, and cinnamon; set aside.

In a large bowl, beat butter, fructose, applesauce, apple juice concentrate, egg substitute, and vanilla with an electric mixer until light and fluffy. Add flour mixture to applesauce mixture and beat until combined. Stir in granola, apples, and cranberries.

Drop by teaspoonfuls about 1 inch apart onto ungreased baking sheets. Bake 20 minutes or until lightly browned. Cool slightly on baking sheet, then remove to a wire rack to cool completely.

KRYSTINE'S
HEALTHY
GOURMET
BAKERY
COOKBOOK

218

LOW-SUGAR
FUDGE BROWNIES

Makes 18 servings

Reduced in fat and sugar, these delectable brownies get their moisture and sweetness from fresh, ripe banana.

PER BROWNIE
Cal 107
Carb 11 gm
Prot 3 gm
Total fat 6 gm
Sat fat 1 gm
Cal from fat 50%
Chol 0 mg
Sodium 148 mg

1 cup reduced-fat margarine
1/2 cup unsweetened cocoa powder
1/3 cup fructose
1/2 cup mashed ripe banana

1 cup egg whites or liquid egg substitute
1 cup unbleached all-purpose flour
1 teaspoon pure vanilla extract
1 cup walnuts (optional), chopped

Preheat oven to 400F (205C). In a large saucepan, melt margarine with cocoa; remove from heat. Stir in fructose, banana, egg whites, and flour and mix thoroughly. Stir in vanilla and walnuts, if using. Pour into a 13 × 9-inch baking pan. Bake 25 to 30 minutes. Cut into 18 pieces.

METRIC CONVERSION CHARTS

Comparison to Metric Measure

When You Know	Symbol	Multiply By	To Find	Symbol
teaspoons	tsp.	5.0	milliliters	ml
tablespoons	tbsp.	15.0	milliliters	ml
fluid ounces	fl. oz.	30.0	milliliters	ml
cups	c	0.24	liters	l
pints	pt.	0.47	liters	l
quarts	qt.	0.95	liters	l
ounces	oz.	28.0	grams	g
pounds	lb.	0.45	kilograms	kg
Fahrenheit	F	5/9 (after subtracting 32)	Celsius	C

Fahrenheit to Celsius

F	C
200–205	95
220–225	105
245–250	120
275	135
300–305	150
325–330	165
345–350	175
370–375	190
400–405	205
425–430	220
445–450	230
470–475	245
500	260

Liquid Measure to Milliliters

1/4 teaspoon	=	1.25 milliliters
1/2 teaspoon	=	2.5 milliliters
3/4 teaspoon	=	3.75 milliliters
1 teaspoon	=	5.0 milliliters
1-1/4 teaspoons	=	6.25 milliliters
1-1/2 teaspoons	=	7.5 milliliters
1-3/4 teaspoons	=	8.75 milliliters
2 teaspoons	=	10.0 milliliters
1 tablespoon	=	15.0 milliliters
2 tablespoons	=	30.0 milliliters

Liquid Measure to Liters

1/4 cup	=	0.06 liters
1/2 cup	=	0.12 liters
3/4 cup	=	0.18 liters
1 cup	=	0.24 liters
1-1/4 cups	=	0.3 liters
1-1/2 cups	=	0.36 liters
2 cups	=	0.48 liters
2-1/2 cups	=	0.6 liters
3 cups	=	0.72 liters
3-1/2 cups	=	0.84 liters
4 cups	=	0.96 liters
4-1/2 cups	=	1.08 liters
5 cups	=	1.2 liters
5-1/2 cups	=	1.32 liters

INDEX